A GOOD BOOK, IN THEORY

ALAN SEARS and JAMES CAIRNS

A GOOD BOOK, IN THEORY

MAKING SENSE THROUGH INQUIRY

THIRD EDITION

UNIVERSITY OF TORONTO PRESS

Higher Education Division

www.utppublishing.com

LIBRARY AND ARCHIVES CANADA CATALOGUING IN PUBLICATION

Sears, Alan, 1956–, author
    A good book, in theory : making sense through inquiry / Alan Sears and James Cairns.—Third edition.

Includes bibliographical references and index.
Issued in print and electronic formats.
ISBN 978-1-4426-0078-2 (bound).—ISBN 978-1-4426-0077-5 (pbk.).—
ISBN 978-1-4426-0013-3 (pdf).—ISBN 978-1-4426-0097-3 (epub)

    1. Critical thinking. 2. Sociology—Philosophy.
I. Cairns, James Irvine, 1979–, author   II. Title.

LB2395.35.S42 2015   301.01   C2014-906633-3
                                            C2014-906634-1

We welcome comments and suggestions regarding any aspect of our publications—please feel free to contact us at news@utphighereducation. com or visit our Internet site at www.utppublishing.com.

North America   UK, Ireland, and continental Europe
5201 Dufferin Street   NBN International
North York, Ontario,   Estover Road, Plymouth, PL6 7PY, UK
Canada, M3H 5T8   ORDERS PHONE: 44 (0) 1752 202301

2250 Military Road   ORDERS FAX: 44 (0) 1752 202333
Tonawanda, New York,   enquiries@nbninternational.com
USA, 14150

ORDERS PHONE: 1–800–565–9523
ORDERS FAX: 1–800–221–9985
ORDERS E-MAIL: utpbooks@utpress.utoronto.ca

The University of Toronto Press acknowledges the financial support for its publishing activities of the Government of Canada through the Canada Book Fund.

Printed in the United States of America

Contents

Thinking Points

Acknowledgements

THANKS TO Anne Brackenbury at the University of Toronto Press, who helped nurture this book from the outset through to this third edition. It was a pleasure to have had this book copyedited twice by Betsy Struthers, who was a true ally in trying to write a book that is interesting to read.

James would like to dedicate this book to Brett Story, whose way of seeing the world makes everything better. The Cairns Bears are an endless source of wisdom, strength, and play. I am grateful for working with insightful and generous colleagues at Laurier Brantford, including Kim Anderson, Tarah Brookfield, Sue Ferguson, Rebecca Godderis, Todd Gordon, Rob Kristofferson, Brenda Murphy, Kate Rossiter, Celine Taillefer-Travers, Kenneth Werbin, and Bonnie Whitlow. Students at Laurier have contributed significantly to my thinking about the importance of social theory. In particular, I'd like to thank Holly Campbell, Alex Denonville, Nick Difelice, Jo-Anne Lawless, Kassi Mead, Kelly Pflug-Back, Jessica Pietryszyn, Mike Rigglesford, and Keyena Smith.

Alan would like to dedicate this book to Ken LeClair. Happy 30th! The book has grown through discussions with Chris Cachia, Kris Erickson, Matt Feagan, Anne Forrest, Terry Gillen, Nicole Neverson, Judy Rebick, Charlene Senn, and Rafeef Ziadah. I particularly thank the students who have challenged me to be a better teacher by modelling independence of thought and action, including Mike Darlington, Daniel Donovan, Kirsten Gaikwad, Emily Guhl, Lowell Hall, Nathan Hammett, Michale Jolaoso, Svetlana Kovtiuh, David Kryszajtys, Azar Masoumi, Mitch Maceachern, Ashley Okoro, Kevin Panton, Steve Rathbone, Steve Richardson, Elsa Silva, Danielle Soulliere, Dustin Soulliere, Pasha Stennett, Cassandra Thompson, and Cheryl Thompson.

Preface: Users' Guide for Students and Instructors

You will probably skip this preface. Lots of us never read the instructions when we buy something new. We just plunge in impatiently and try to figure it out on the go. Prefaces are like instruction manuals for books, so we often ignore them and get right into the reading. At times, however, we regret our impatience because we can't figure something out on our own. Sometimes there are useful things to learn from instructions.

Of course, books usually do not need a users' guide. This book is, however, rather different from most of the theory texts that are available, so we thought it might be helpful to say a bit about why we wrote it and how it might be useful.

THE ORIGIN STORY OF THIS BOOK

This book grew directly out of our teaching experiences in postsecondary institutions. Alan wrote the first edition of the book after teaching compulsory theory courses for over 15 years. Students had to take these courses to meet the requirements for their degree. Over time, Alan became convinced that he was doing something wrong. The students forced to take those courses told him in written evaluations that he did a fairly good job of making dry material somewhat interesting. But they were not convinced that there was a very good reason for these theory courses to be compulsory. These courses did not succeed at developing students' appetites for theoretical thinking; they did not convince students that anything they learned here could be useful in their futures.

In retrospect, Alan realized that his general approach has been to introduce students to a set of social theories without ever providing any guide to theoretical thinking itself. As a result, students in those courses drew on their prior educational experience and tried to approach theories in a fact-like way, learning by rote, for example, that Marx wrote about class struggle and Durkheim about the division of labour. But the courses did not equip them to understand why that distinction might matter. A small number of students worked it out for themselves, but many others never saw the usefulness of theory courses.

Alan went back to his own experience of postsecondary education to help identify this problem. He took five years off between getting a three-year BA and returning for a fourth year before applying to graduate school. He got really nervous when he returned to classes because he had retained virtually nothing. He could remember vaguely, for example, that Durkheim and Weber both did comparisons of Catholics and Protestants, but, beyond that, he did not have a clue about their major contributions. He was afraid that he was entering fourth-year courses with almost no memory of the prerequisite courses he had taken along the way.

Yet, that fourth year proved to be much easier than the previous three. Alan realized pretty quickly that retaining the specific, detailed content of the courses he had already taken was not that important as this content was fairly easy to learn again. He *had* learned something important in his first three years of university, but it was not the detailed content. Rather, although he wasn't fully aware of it at the time, he had begun to acquire ways of doing systemic inquiry. He had developed an approach to learning that included methods for reading, writing, analysing texts, listening to teachers, and engaging in discussion. Those methods were more important to his survival in fourth year than the facts he had memorized for exams and forgotten long ago, usually within moments of completing the final. His years in the workforce helped him develop a confidence and sense of purpose that, together with the methods learned previously, allowed him to thrive the year he returned.

So Alan set out to write a book that focused on the method of theoretical thinking rather than on the specific details of particular schools of social thought. The process of writing this book also got him more interested in questions of learning and teaching at the postsecondary level. In that context, he was asked to work with others (Matt Feagan, Kris Erickson, and Chris Cachia) to develop workshops that would help teaching assistants hone their craft. James participated in one of those workshops near the end of his PhD studies.

That's how the two of us met. We ended up having a lot of conversations about learning and teaching and, ultimately, got the chance to co-instruct a first-year course using this book.

Our experience of using this book in a large introductory course convinced us that it would be helpful to write a second edition. The purpose of the course was to introduce first-year students from a number of disciplines to social science inquiry. We were encouraged by the ways in which the first edition of the book helped students learn about formal theoretical thinking, but, at different points in the semester, we found ourselves wishing that the book had expanded on the relationship between theorizing and empirical research. We decided that more could have been said about the cycle of inquiry that moves between fact-finding and explanation. This cycle was often discussed in our classes—why wasn't it explored in greater detail in the book? Teaching has a funny way of clarifying ideas that we thought we already understood.

From the start of our new project, we wanted to preserve the first edition's focus on theoretical thinking and to ensure that the book remained relevant for theory courses. At the same time, we wanted to add further discussion on the relationship of theoretical thinking to methodical research in processes of inquiry. Understanding this connection is an important part of theory education, but it is also relevant for learning research methods and for introducing social science as a specific way of knowing.

We agreed to work as a team to rewrite the book. Although we share many of the same interests—in teaching, social theory, political journalism, and sushi, although not always in the same sorts of music—we also bring different strengths and experiences to writing this book. James brings the experience of using the text to teach a course on social science inquiry, as well as a background in interdisciplinary studies. His training in political science, communication studies, and cultural studies offered a fresh take on a project—one that addresses basic questions about the promises and limitations of academic ways of knowing.

Further, James brought a passion for teaching that he could trace back to being raised in a family of deeply committed teachers. The craft of teaching intrigued him from the outset, and he put a lot of thought into ways of engaging students so that they developed an active approach to learning. He also brought to the classroom a deep interest in music, theatre, reading, and cultural production that added tools to reflecting on different ways of knowing and interacting.

Co-teaching, with the two of us in the classroom at the same time, provided a very different experience of the professor role, challenging the idea of teaching as an individual performance. Similarly, co-writing opened up the writing process in new ways, as we collaborated to map out plans, draft sections, and rework each other's words. The experience of collaboration itself has reshaped this book. In this edition, we have shifted the voice of the book away from the very personal first-person ("I") perspective that Alan used in the first edition and we kept in the second. This has been a bit of a challenge, as the first person plural ("we") has a certain ambiguity when used in writing. It can refer to the writers of the book, but also, at a more general level, to all of us ("We all think theoretically in our everyday lives"). Further, we (James and Alan) do have different stories, preferences, and perspectives. But, ultimately, we thought that the collaborative experience was best expressed with the use of "we" in this book. We hope you can negotiate easily between the general and specific use of "we."

This third edition has offered us the chance to address gaps in the second. James has ended up doing much of his teaching in the area of theory and methods, which provided him with different insights into how this book worked. Specifically, we decided to add more discussion of postmodern theories and a richer engagement with Indigenous ways of knowing. We also wanted to work more on the overall flow of the book and to add in some activities that might help guide the application of concepts we use.

THEORETICAL THINKING
AND ACTIVE INQUIRY

THIS BOOK sets out a different approach to teaching and learning theory. The focus here is on the role of theoretical thinking as one aspect of a larger cycle of inquiry—a cycle that moves between using our senses to explore the world around us and seeking explanations for events through the identification of general patterns. Theoretical thinking begins with the everyday theorizing we all do to make sense of the world around us. As we go through our lives, every one of us develops working assumptions based on various forms of generalization from our experience, assumptions that we use as a guide to the situations we face. Without these, we would be completely at sea when we confront anything new or different.

These generalizations are based on our ability to distinguish the aspects that are specific to a particular situation from those that are more likely to recur. When a bug crawls out of a piece of pie we are eating in a restaurant, we seek out ways to avoid repeating this disgusting experience. As a result, we have to figure out the general pattern of bug appearance so that we might alter our behaviour to reduce the possibility of this recurring. We could generalize that pies are likely to be bug-infested and so avoid pie for the rest of our lives. But this decision would go against a lifetime of eating bug-less pies; that is, our generalization would contradict the bulk of our experiences. The theory would not fit the facts. Or we might assume that the restaurant had hygiene problems and so avoid that one place. We learn to identify the features that define a particular phenomenon as exceptional rather than as part of a more general trend.

The generalizations we develop through our everyday theoretical thinking are extremely useful but tend also to be limited in their power because they draw only on our own insights and what we have gleaned from others. The formal theories developed in scholarly study and through social movement activism often have a penetrating power because they reflect a broader view developed through interchange over time and a live up to a more rigorous set of requirements for internal consistency and fit with the world. Although sometimes it seems as though people who write theory are primarily concerned about little more than proving themselves right and proving others wrong, formal theories are powerful because of their ability to shed light upon the way the world works. This ability is not magic; however, it is no mind trick or lucky guess either. Rather, thinking theoretically is about making sense of the facts before us and using our theories to pursue new facts.

This book illustrates some of the power of these more formal theories with reference to issues in our surroundings. The aim is to show how the world we already know can look very different through the lens of particular theories, just as looking through binoculars can provide new insights on a hike through the woods. It is a guide to theoretical thinking, which is one important and often neglected dimension of theory education and of courses on how to do research. The aim is to help readers develop a method that will assist them in making sense of the specific theories they will be exposed to through their education by relating theoretical thinking to their own activities in the world. It builds on the foundation of the everyday theorizing we all engage in all the time. The tone is a bit more chatty and informal than in most theory texts. The aim of the book is to complement rather than replace other texts that provide a detailed introduction to specific theorists and schools of thought.

Our interest in theory education stems from our shared conviction that theoretical thinking is extremely useful in the world. Theory might seem to be the most obscure and academic of subjects, particularly given its specialized vocabulary, which is difficult to penetrate and its big concepts, which can seem pretty far removed from reality. Yet it can be practical, providing vital insights that allow us to make sense of the world around us and that serve as a guide to action when we try to do something about the things we would like to change.

Theory provides us with visions of the world that go well beyond the comprehension we are able to develop through our daily activities. Malls, for example, have become major fixtures in the lives of many of us, whether we work, shop, go to movies, hang out, or eat there. Different theories allow us to see the growth of the mall over the last 50 years as one of a series of interrelated changes that have had a huge effect on our leisure, work, and political activities.

Leisure activities have tended to become much more dependent on the consumption of products we buy rather than on the things we do and create on our own or for each other. Music, for example, is something we experience mainly through recordings. Birthday parties are increasingly held at fast food restaurants or activity centres rather than at home. Shopping has become a leisure activity in its own right, rather than a means to an end (the actual purchase of something you need).

Contending theories provide very different explanations for these changes: they might be taken as signs of a generally affluent society in which most people now have access to considerable wealth, or they might be attributed to the spread of consumerism that increasingly encourages us to define our self-worth according to the products we can buy. Each of these theoretical perspectives will highlight certain aspects of the phenomenon under consideration and, at least by implication, suggest certain forms of action. Should you sign a petition against the arrival of a new Walmart in town or rush out to enjoy new access to cheaper products? Your theory of shopping in our current society will have something to do with your response. Of course, no theory of shopping, malls, music, or anything else can be dreamed up independently from experience. Although it is true that contending theories seek to draw generalizations that go beyond our daily activities, they are always embedded in processes of inquiry that are crucially informed by the observation and documentation of human life in action.

THEORY OF TEACHING AND LEARNING

THIS BOOK promotes the approach of thinking through theory by applying it. One important body of theory that we applied in writing this book examined learning in the classroom. Teachers often take the form of classroom learning for granted and teach by drawing on the model of the way their own education was structured. Similarly, people draw on the patterns they have been exposed to, whether consciously or not, in the realms of parenting and couple relationships and in other aspects of life.

The process of teaching as we were taught is being interrupted in the postsecondary environment by a range of debates that are coming to a head in the early twenty-first century. There are widespread claims that traditional approaches to university teaching are offering diminishing returns in the current context. Indeed, the development of information technology and online education raises questions about whether the classroom is even necessary at all.

This book is designed as a tool to help in the development of an active classroom environment. One model of this that has some currency is the "flipped classroom," in which students watch lectures online at their leisure and spend class time processing information in active ways. This book is an attempt to flip the pedagogy of theory education from information transfer to active application.

The active classroom raises the vexing question of class size. University classes are large and tend to be growing. It is much easier to imagine active learning in the context of a smaller seminar class in which interaction is at least somewhat more comfortable and participants actually get to meet each other. However, we are convinced that it is possible to engage students in active learning in a large class (e.g., over 150 students), and we have done so using this book. We make extensive use of small group activities, reflective writing, and problem-solving exercises in the classroom.

Too often, theory is taught in a highly academic form, sealed off from the everyday world and from a real connection to practical activity or the lived experiences of students. As a result, theory courses, from a student's perspective, do not seem essential even if they are required. Every student knows they will never be asked a question about the psycho-analytic theory of Jacques Lacan in a future (non-academic) job interview.

We wrote this book as a tool to assist in teaching theory differently. The book can be used as a jumping-off point at the beginning of a theory course—to help newcomers to the subject develop an appetite and aptitude for theoretical thinking before facing the challenge of handling the complex theories written by the big names. Alternatively, instructors could choose to assign various chapters here and there throughout a course, creating a back-and-forth pattern between the study of formal theories written at a high level of abstraction and a more grounded approach to theoretical thinking.

The book uses one theoretical debate—between the social order and conflict models of theory—to demonstrate the importance and vitality of theoretical analysis. We selected this particular debate as it closely parallels key themes in contemporary discussions of social and political issues, ranging from moral values to work processes and from social welfare to the status of women. We do not claim this debate exhausts the field of theoretical interchange, but we hope that using a more simplified debate format to introduce students to theoretical thinking will allow them an entry point into what is sometimes an overwhelming array of theoretical choices. The aim here is to prepare students with a strong base from which they can negotiate the complex and disputed terrain of contemporary social theory. We have deliberately problematized this debate format by showing how the whole social order versus conflict frame can be critiqued from the perspectives of Indigenous ways of knowing and postmodernism.

This book can also be useful in courses not focused exclusively on the study of social theory. One of our primary goals is to elaborate on what it means to theorize as part of a process of methodical inquiry. In introductory courses, theoretical thinking can challenge students to think of disciplines as ways of seeing the world rather than as massive vaults piled high with collections of facts accumulated in previous research. The goal is to get students to begin to use disciplinary perspectives to frame their own analysis of the world around them, so they can begin to understand the practical value of the subjects they are studying in illuminating their environment directly or indirectly.

We also see a need for a better bridge between theory and methods courses. Most postsecondary curricula do not make it easy for students to understand the role of theory in the research process. Sure, we might offer some formalized statements about beginning with hypotheses derived from theory, but, nevertheless, we tend to present research methods as technical problems quite distinct from theoretical thinking. In order to reinforce the idea that theory and method are, in fact, complementary features of a particular way of learning about the world, the new chapter in this edition of the book situates theoretical thinking within a larger process of inquiry. Because it suggests that theoretical thinking is impoverished without rigorous research and that even the most technically perfect research project will yield little without an analysis grounded in powerful theoretical insights, the book could be used in theory or methods courses to draw the link between explanation and documentation.

This book could also be useful in assisting students to understand the importance of theory in courses that don't teach theory or method, primarily. We find students often consider theory an intrusion in a course on crime, international development, or labour studies. They often hope for an unbiased perspective that will shed light on a particular area of our social existence. It is our sense that we often fail to explain the importance of theoretical analysis in studying various subjects. Theoretical thinking frames our view of the subject, whether we are conscious of our presuppositions or not. This book encourages self-reflection as a necessary tool to become more aware of our own presuppositions, as well as analysis in order to figure out those of others.

We hope that this book helps students see theoretical thinking as the development of something they already do rather than as an alien activity they can never master. Thus, the book may be useful in a variety of courses. The ultimate goal is to help students assume a more active role in their own education, seeing the things they learn as the development of their own aptitudes rather than as something external that they are forced to try to assimilate.

To that end, we have included activities and thinking points throughout the book, to help readers apply to the world around them the concepts they learn here. We designed these also to help teachers think of classroom activities that might challenge students in their classes to use theory actively—as part of a process of problem solving.

IN PARTING

WE HOPE you have fun with this book. We think theory is a hoot. Sure, some of the reading is hard and maybe even tedious at times. Still, theory can be exciting because it allows us to be surprised by a world we thought we already knew. It makes us think in depth about cooking or football, work or fast food. This book is designed to help you play with theory, using it the way a funhouse mirror makes the familiar strange. These effects can be disturbing, as you see yourself and your everyday world reflected in ways that seem distorted and off-putting. This discomfort is a necessary part of the process that leads us to learn by inquiring about the circumstances that shape our experiences.

Anthropologists use the term "culture shock" to describe the sense of dislocation that comes from being immersed in an unfamiliar setting. They seek out such experiences rather than avoiding them, even though culture shock can be very painful. We can be enriched by stretching ourselves to understand things that might at first seem threatening because they are different from what we expect. Theoretical thinking can produce a kind of culture shock when we look at ourselves and our surroundings. It allows us to know our familiar world in new ways.

I

An Interesting Idea,
In Theory

THEORY HAS a bad reputation. It can seem rather useless and is often very hard to understand. Indeed, the words "in theory" are often used to describe idealized thinking that does not fit with reality. For example, in the play *The Bald Soprano* by Eugène Ionesco (1958, 22–23), two English couples, the Smiths and the Martins, are sitting around chatting. The doorbell rings twice. Each time, Mrs. Smith goes to the door and returns to announce that no one is there. Then it rings a third time.

Mr. Smith asks his wife to answer it. But Mrs. Smith says she will not. "The first time there was no one. The second time, no one. Why do you think there is someone there now?"

Mr. Smith explains, "As for me, when I go to visit someone, I ring in order to be admitted. I think that everyone does the same thing and that each time there is a ring there must be someone there."

Mrs. Smith responds, "This is true in theory. But in reality things happen differently. You have just seen otherwise."

This dialogue is a wonderful summary of common everyday assumptions about theory. Trust your senses; what you *see* is the *real* truth. The idea that someone must be at the door if the bell has rung is only true *in theory*, in an idealized system of thought that does not necessarily correspond to reality.

We have written this book to convey our enthusiasm for theory and challenge its bad reputation. Theory is not simply an obscure mind-game played by clever academics who have nothing better to do with their time. In fact, **theoretical**

thinking is absolutely essential to our daily lives. Richard Hyman (1975, 2) argues that people cannot act without theory, "for theory is a way of seeing, of understanding, and of planning." At its core, theoretical thinking is about generalization, relating a new situation to an old one in order to discern patterns and figure out what is likely to happen.

Both Mr. and Mrs. Smith used theoretical thinking in *The Bald Soprano*. Mr. Smith developed a general law of doorbells from his own experience: "Each time there is a ring, there must be someone there." A bit later in the scene, Mrs. Smith derived her own general law: "Experience teaches us that when one hears the doorbell ring, it is because there is never anyone there."

The Smiths' theoretical thinking is essentially practical—it guides them to action when the doorbell rings. It is grounded in their immediate experience. It is also flawed, in that they both construct a universal rule to cover all circumstances out of a very narrow base of experience. Of course, we all do this frequently and then refine the broad generalizations when they do not fit reality. We also supplement these generalizations from our own experience with things we learn from others, either in the form of anecdotes that relate snippets of their experiences or as theoretical statements, whether formal or informal.

Unfortunately, the study of **formal theories** within **academic disciplines** usually makes no connection to this practical **everyday theorizing** that is grounded in experience. Instead, the study often begins with the complex and powerful theories that have been developed in various disciplines over generations. The reference point for such study is often other theories, rather than experience. Students might learn to distinguish Karl Marx from Max Weber but might not learn why that distinction matters.

We love theory because it is so useful in acting on the world. We believe it helps us gain power over the world by providing us with insights for understanding the way things work. Yet we sometime fear, as theory teachers, that we've failed to convince students that theory is useful in any way.

The formal theories we teach seem to have nothing to do with the everyday understanding of life that we all use to guide our activity.

Our aim in this book is to show that theory is useful by using it to shed a new light on everyday experience. We want to help you to use theoretical thinking to examine your environment and your own assumptions in new ways. We also want to help you think about the role that theory plays within a larger **cycle of inquiry** and how gathering facts (or documentation) and theorizing (or explaining) can be made to work together in order to help us understand the world. In the next chapter, we will talk more about the formal theoretical models used in academic research. Chapter 3 places these models in the context of a broader "cycle of inquiry" and looks at academic research as a particular type of rigorous inquiry. In Chapter 4, we will begin an examination of our environment and assumptions right where you are—by looking at the classroom and its social relations. Then, in Chapter 5, we will examine the real world you might assume exists outside of the ivory towers of academia. Chapter 6 considers ideas about nature in contemporary society. In Chapter 7, we will look at the way theoretical work casts light on the use of time in our everyday lives.

We have chosen these topics to map a route that proceeds from where you are to the very broad generalizations that are the building blocks of formal theorizing. The book is designed as a series of theoretical questions that follow one another. Why is the classroom organized this way? Why do we assume that the "real" world is beyond the walls of the classroom? Why does this relationship between the classroom and the "real" world seem natural, so we assume that this is just the way things are? Is the passage of time the most natural of all human experiences, or is it socially constructed in very different ways in various societies?

In doing so, we set up a dialogue between the everyday theoretical thinking you have already done about these topics and the formal theories associated with academic disciplines. We will try to convince you that these formal theories are worth getting to know, even if they "play hard to get" and seem to have no "social skills." Everyday theorizing is the crucial basis for all theoretical thinking, but, as we shall see, it can be enriched by engagement with the formal theories that have been developed over time.

THINGS FALL DOWN, IN THEORY

CHANCES ARE you already know something about the laws of gravity. You know which way that precious but ugly vase that was once your great-grandmother's will go if it slips from your hands. You probably know also the name Isaac Newton. In the folk myth about Newton, he was sitting under a tree one day when an apple fell on his head. Being a great thinker, he generalized this into the law of gravity: things fall down.

Of course, if you think about it for a moment, it is obvious that, before Newton developed his theory, people knew that things fall down. Newton did not invent the idea of falling to the ground. That vase would not have drifted upwards before his time, nor would anyone have expected that it should. Newton's contribution was a theory of gravity that explained why and how things fall. This theory contributes to people's abilities to act on the world, making bridges stand up or sending satellites into space.

We might assume that scientific advance is the result of greater precision in observation and measurement. Telescopes and microscopes give us the capacity to see farther or in greater detail. However, it is only theory that allows us to explain the phenomena we observe. The great advances of science are associated with new theoretical developments that allow us to envision the universe and our place in it in new ways.

Charles Darwin did not invent the idea of the evolution of species. His own grandfather had worked on evolutionary theories, as did many earlier thinkers. Darwin's great leap was to develop a particular theoretical account that explained how and why evolution occurred over time. His account focused on the *process* of natural selection. The reproduction of new generations includes a certain amount of random variation, meaning that occasional glitches in the process of reproduction yield a mutation that has slightly different characteristics. Darwin theorized that those characteristics that allowed a species to thrive in its particular environment were most likely to be passed on, as the individuals so endowed were most likely to survive and reproduce.

Before Darwin, the French thinker Jean-Baptiste Lamarck developed a theoretical approach to evolution that was highly influential. Lamarck's approach suggested that characteristics acquired during the life of an individual could be passed on to his or her offspring, so that a deer that developed muscles through running a lot might pass that down to the next generation. Darwin and Lamarck, then, developed competing theoretical accounts that provided very different ways of understanding the process of evolution. These differences were fought out in sharp theoretical debates over a long period of time.

IN MY OPINION, MR. DARWIN, YOUR THEORY SUCKS

THE DIFFERENCE between Lamarck and Darwin was not simply a difference of opinion. One of the most difficult things to understand in the discussion of theoretical thinking is the relationship between **theory, opinion,** and **fact.** We will start with dictionary definitions for these terms while cautioning you from the outset that, in social theory, terms are often used in a technical sense not always captured in general-use dictionaries. Nevertheless, dictionary definitions are enormously useful, and one of the most important aspects of theoretical thinking is the careful use of words.

A theory, according to the *New Oxford Dictionary of English*, is "a supposition or a system of ideas intended to explain something, especially one based on general principles independent of the things to be explained" (Oxford 2001, 1922). In other words, a theory provides an explanation of a phenomenon that uses some sort of broader framework of understanding. This framework cannot simply offer a description of the phenomenon as an explanation. For example, it is not a theory of evolution to say that, over time, the characteristics of species change so they are more in tune with the environment. The theoretical aspect is the explanation of *how* this change occurs and refers to broader scientific frameworks used for understanding life forms.

An opinion, in contrast, is "a view or judgement formed about something, not necessarily based on fact or knowledge" (Oxford 2001, 1301). Opinions are deeply personal, depending on our tastes, feelings, and ideas about the world. Opinions do not need to be based on any particular claims to expertise. Even though he hardly watches it, Alan tells James that baseball is boring ("Because it *is* so boring!!!" says Alan); and James tells Alan that baseball is thrilling and Alan is missing out on one of summer's greatest gifts. We've repeated these arguments on numerous occasions, and neither of us is yet to be moved the slightest bit by the opinion of the other.

Finally, a fact is "a thing that is indisputably the case" (Oxford 2001, 657). People claim that facts are beyond dispute when they are based on **empirical data**, the information gained through the use of our five senses. In principle, as least, we can resolve a dispute about the facts by using our sight, hearing, smell, taste, or touch. The term "fact" involves a claim that the phenomenon in question exists outside of your head and is therefore accessible to your senses. That facts are external does not mean, however, that we will easily agree on them. In *theory*, facts are indisputable, though in *reality*, we argue about them all the time.

This all seems quite simple so far. The problem is that facts, opinions, and theories get all mixed up in discussions and debates. Indeed, in everyday discussions we often fail to distinguish between differences in fact, opinion, or theory. When the fans of two competing teams argue about tomorrow's game, there is a fairly good chance that this will include disputes over facts, opinions, and theories. The score the last time the two teams met is a fact, though each side's supporters might remember it differently. Your claim that our star player is an overpaid bum is an opinion. The statement that our team has the best defence might involve elements of theory, if we relate it to a broader analysis of effective strategy for defensive play.

In the more formal setting of academic disciplines, we are supposed to be quite clear about the relationship between theory, fact, and opinion. Clarity can, however, be quite difficult to achieve, particularly given that opinion influences our preference for certain theories. Each theory is founded on key premises, cornerstone assumptions about the way things work. These assumptions are inseparable from beliefs about the way things should be. There is, therefore, a political dimension to theoretical work, as theories frame our vision of the world as it was, is, and might be.

For example, when Charles Darwin was a student in the 1820s, evolutionary theory in Britain was largely the domain of political and social radicals. It challenged the idea of a god-given natural order in which everything had its place. Thus, it was futile and destructive for the wretched of the earth to question their place in the world. The proponents of evolutionary theory challenged these ideas of a fixed and god-given natural and social order.

Darwin was not a radical in this political sense. Indeed, Adrian Desmond and James Moore (1991, xviii) argue, he sat on his evolutionary theories for a long time before publishing them as he was afraid of their radical implications at a time of social upheaval in Britain. Stephen J. Gould (1977) points out that Darwin delayed publishing his theories for over 20 years and, even after their publication, tried to downplay the philosophical implications of his scientific analysis.

The debate between Lamarckian and Darwinian ideas of evolution also had political dimensions. Lamarck was a French scientist, associated in the eyes of British conservatives with the French Revolution and the overthrow of that country's old order. Further, Lamarck's theory of evolution suggested that progress rather than order was the central theme of nature, as living things could develop new capacities in their lifetime and pass these on to offspring. If our activities or diet make us stronger or taller than our parents, then it is possible that these characteristics might be passed on to our children.

In contrast, Darwin argued that it was only inherited characteristics, and not those developed through activities over a lifetime, that mattered in the process of evolution. A particular moth might be more likely to survive and reproduce in a smoggy urban setting than others of the same species as the result of an accident in the act of reproduction that happened to make it a bit darker than normal. The progress made by individuals over their lifespan had no impact on the evolutionary path of the species; what mattered were only accidents of reproduction that have nothing to do with any desire for improvement. Darwin developed this theory of evolution in counterposition to Lamarck and his radical followers (Desmond and Moore 1991, 315). Indeed, his vision of the natural world was deeply influenced by his reading of the conservative theorist Malthus, who argued that humans are in a struggle for existence in the face of scarcity as population grows at a faster rate than resources (Gould 1977, 21–22).

The debate between Darwinian and Lamarckian theories of evolution had important political dimensions, but that does not mean it can be reduced to opinions. It would not be very convincing to claim that Darwin's theory sucks or to attack him personally. Theoretical debate, particularly in more formal situations such as academic discussion, is based on arguments that meet certain internal and external tests. Internally, the argument should be consistent and coherent, so that the various conclusions flow logically from the premises. Externally, the argument should fit the facts, so that it should accurately predict the way things actually unfold. If our theory of antigravity predicts that we will float towards the ceiling as soon as we unwrap our legs from the supports of the chairs we rest on, then we'll see when we test it and let go, that our theory doesn't fit the facts. Of course, the facts themselves are often debatable, given that there are many possibilities for errors of measurement or interpretation.

Gould (2000, 116) claims that Lamarck's model of evolution fits the facts in explaining cultural change in human societies better than Darwin's. He argues that social change has particular properties that make it a special case within the broader realm of change within nature. Specifically, we can develop new cultural capacities in our lifetime and pass them on to the next generation. Alan grew up in a country where polio had been largely eliminated by vaccination while his parents lived through polio epidemics that saw kids confined to their own backyards. The knowledge to prevent polio is a cultural legacy developed in one generation and passed down to the next. At the same time, it is not true that the physical characteristics that individuals develop during their lifetime can be passed on genetically. An individual who lifts weights to build muscle does not change her or his genetic code in such a way as to produce more muscular offspring. Lamarck thus seems to fit the facts in explaining cultural change while Darwin fits the facts in explaining biological evolution.

One of the most important skills you can develop in a course on **methodical inquiry** is the ability to unpack arguments, that is, to distinguish facts from opinions and theories and to explain how the information in an argument was collected and interpreted in the first place. This analytical skill will enable you to be much more persuasive, improving your ability to convince people to do things your way at work, to challenge an unfair division of chores at home, or to do well in your course assignments. Learning theories and identifying the role of theory within the cycle of inquiry is a crucial way to improve your analytical abilities, just as lifting weights increases your physical strength. For many people, lifting weights is a means to an end, a way to develop the strength that is required in other activities such as running, swimming, or playing football. Similarly, training in theories will develop your abilities at critical thinking and persuasion, even if you do not develop an abiding interest in theoretical debate in and of itself.

Thinking Point: Facts and Assumptions

Doing methodical inquiry involves being very clear about what you know for certain, what assumptions you're making, and what you don't know. Distinguishing between facts, assumptions, and unknowns might seem easy to do at first, but, as you begin making sharp distinctions among them, this process can become more complicated. To get a feel for what it's like to make these distinctions, look at the photo on this page and make a list of the following:

- What do you know about the image for certain (in other words, what facts about it can you name)?
- What do you not know but can reasonably assume, based on the facts that you have?
- What do you not know but might want to find out in order to better understand the photograph?

As a result of doing this exercise, can you make any generalizations about the relationship between facts, assumptions, and unknowns or the process of identifying them? If you were examining a real event, as opposed to a photograph in a book, how might the process of distinguishing facts, assumptions, and unknowns be different?

Figure 1.1

FIND YOUR VOICE, IN THEORY

Perhaps the loftiest goal of education is that all students gain new capacities to express themselves through their learning. The Women's Studies Program at the University of Windsor expresses this aim in a wonderful slogan: "Find Your Voice." Sadly, many students lose their voices in the classroom. They may feel they have nothing to say about the topic at hand, which usually seems to have little to do with their own lives or experiences. Further, they may feel judged in a setting where it seems that the instructor is always evaluating and categorizing students. They actually find it hard to speak aloud in that setting, feeling a strain that makes it hard to get words out.

Keath Fraser (2002) was forced to think about the issue of voice when he developed a physiological condition that made his vocal chords go into spasms, choking his ability to speak. The condition first showed up in the classroom, where he experienced "an unfathomable acceleration of pulse, and a heart that thrashed at my chest wall like a crazed crow, before the inevitable sound of someone deeply troubled, deeply *flawed*, emerged from my throat when I was asked to read aloud" (Fraser 2002, 11). He assumed that this voice disturbance in class was a sign of personal failure. Eventually, he found out that this condition was physiological and could be treated by injections.

The voice is a funny thing. It has a mental dimension as the expression of thoughts, and, at the same time, it has a physical one, the action of forcing air through vocal chords formed into a particular shape. These two aspects of voice are totally interconnected. For example, a voice expert consulted by Fraser (2002, 33) noted a similarity in pattern between stuttering and his own condition, called spasmodic dysphonia. Both these conditions had physiological dimensions, yet they tended to be triggered by "authority figures, having to speak in public, or before a group." They were less likely to be triggered by "speaking to underlings and children, to people you know rather than strangers, singing."

Finding your voice is more difficult when you are speaking up to power than in a situation of equality or one where you have the power. The classroom is built around an unequal power structure, as we will discuss in Chapter 4. It is therefore a particular challenge to find your voice in this setting, as classroom discussion seldom includes the expertise you have accumulated through your own life experience.

The loss of voice inside the classroom is often severe for those whose experience is most distant from the perspective generally offered from the front of the room. Himani Bannerji (1995, 57) powerfully discusses the experience of being cast as an "outsider" in university classes:

> Often I was the only non-white student in these classes. . . .
> They carried on discussions as though I was not there, or
> if I made a comment . . . the flow would be interrupted.
> Then they would look at each other and teachers would
> wait in the distance for me to finish.

The development of insiders and outsiders in the classroom is usually not a conscious activity. Professors and teachers often make an effort to be scrupulously fair. Yet lurking beneath this fairness are unconscious assumptions about what is important and what we in the room all share in the way of experience.

Dionne Brand (2001, 24–25) argues that the everyday world of contemporary black people in the Americas is haunted by the historical experience of being violently removed from their places of origin and forced into slavery in another ("new") world. She refers to this forced removal as the "Door of No Return," the experience of coerced displacement that eliminates any possible return.

> Black experience in any modern city or town in the
> Americas is a haunting. One enters a room and history
> follows; one enters a room and history precedes. History
> is already seated in the chair in the empty room when one
> arrives. Where one stands in society seems always related
> to this historical experience.

Yet this sense of loss, of the violent expropriation of self and community, is seldom if ever made a central feature of the shared understandings in the classroom, for reasons that will be discussed in Chapter 4. Similarly, the specific life experiences of women, working-class people, and lesbians, gays, bisexuals, or transgendered people are only rarely addressed in this context.

In this book, we are arguing that learning theory should be about finding your voice, about expressing yourself in theory. That means your opinions and experiences are necessary but not sufficient parts of this learning process. The challenge is to work your own thinking into an analytical perspective that provides you with a framework to engage with formal theories.

THEORY AND COMMON SENSE

THE ITALIAN theorist Antonio Gramsci (1971, 323) argues that "everyone is a philosopher, though in his own way and unconsciously." Our thoughts and actions are based on sets of assumptions about the way the world works. We act on the basis of expectations, which we generate through theoretical work that is often unconscious, generalizing from past experiences to model new situations and develop appropriate responses.

Gramsci used the term **common sense** to describe everyday philosophizing as opposed to conscious theoretical thinking. Our common-sense assumptions tend to be an eclectic blend of personal tastes and opinions; wisdom received from family, friends, or other influential individuals; and knowledge obtained from schools, religious institutions, political leaders, media, and other social institutions. We tend not to worry too much if the various bits of common-sense knowledge we have built up are not processed to the extent that they fit together into a tidy package that is consistent and coherent in any rigorous sense.

Gramsci was a **Marxist** activist who saw theory as an important component of freedom struggles. The undigested common sense we pick up here and there in our lives most often confirms the sense that the current world order is the only possible kind of social arrangement. He thought it was necessary, therefore, to break with this common sense in order to begin working towards a different kind of society, and doing both requires serious theoretical work. For Gramsci, then, it was crucial that theoretical thinking not be confined to an elite but, rather, that it be opened up to become everyone's domain. Everyone must be offered the opportunity to think critically about the world, even to the extent of reflecting critically on our own common-sense assumptions. Gramsci (1971, 323) argues that it is better to

> work out consciously and critically one's own conception of the world and thus, in connection with the labours of one's own brain, choose one's sphere of activity, take an active part in the creation of the history of the world, be one's own guide.

The aim of this book is to invite you to use theoretical thinking to be your own guide. Theory can help you develop your capacities to act in the world to achieve personal, economic, or political goals. Clear thinking is not an obscure academic exercise but a crucial skill that will make you more effective in the world.

MAKING THE FAMILIAR STRANGE

ONE OF the key requirements for clear theoretical thinking is that we become aware of the taken-for-granted, common-sense assumptions that generally frame our vision of the world. The sense that we already know the essentials is one of the greatest obstacles to critical thinking. Indeed, Terry Eagleton (1990, 34) argues that children often make very good critical thinkers as their way of seeing the world is not yet framed by deeply integrated assumptions about the ways of the world.

> Children make the best theorists, since they have not yet been educated into accepting our routine social practice as "natural" and so insist on posing to those practices the most embarrassingly general and fundamental questions, regarding them with a wondering estrangement which we adults have long forgotten.

Unfortunately, we adults cannot simply take on a childlike innocence and walk around asking naïve questions. We have integrated assumptions about the world so deeply into our selves throughout our lives that we cannot separate our own perspective from what is actually out there.

Effective theoretical work therefore requires a particular kind of self-reflection in which we become more aware of the frameworks we use to make sense of the world. The German playwright Bertolt Brecht (1964, 144) thinks that one step in the development of this kind of awareness is to make the familiar strange: "Before familiarity can turn into awareness the familiar must be stripped of its inconspicuousness; we must give up assuming that the object in question needs no explanation."

A good theorist assumes every phenomenon needs explanation and rejects the idea that the workings of the world are self-evident and **natural**. Even an everyday sunset can stimulate us to think about the ways in which we know reality. John Berger (1972, 7–9) writes, "Each evening we *see* the sun set. We *know* the earth is turning away from it. Yet the knowledge, the explanation, never quite fits the sight." The sun looks as if it is moving, even if you have learned that the earth is actually rotating around it.

Defamiliarization, looking at things we already know as if for the first time, is an important feature of theoretical thinking. It is necessary for effective analysis to ask basic questions about an everyday reality we already think we know. Theoretical thinking requires that we hunt relentlessly for the actual causes of the phenomena we experience, even if we think we already know the answer.

STANDPOINT MATTERS

Of course, we do not all begin the search for causes and explanations from exactly the same place. Surely a banker getting rich from interest on student loans sees debt very differently than do students owing thousands of dollars to the bank.

Just as prison walls look very different depending on whether they're being viewed through the eyes of a warden or an inmate, where we stand in the world shapes our view of society.

The social theorist Nancy Hartsock (1998) wrote about "the feminist standpoint." She argued that the viewpoint of women offers a unique and crucial perspective on gender inequality. The simple walk through a campus at night after an evening class generally feels very different for women and men. Women tend to see a threat of violence whereas men generally do not. From the position of women, then, the campus actually looks different. Though Hartsock recognized that sexism is not the same for all women, she argued that important social patterns can be seen more clearly from the perspective of women and other marginalized people. Where you stand can make some things easier to see while blocking other features of the landscape.

In 2014, the Associated Press conducted a poll asking Americans whether the Washington Redskins football team should change its name. More than 80 per cent said "No," the name is fine as is. By contrast, dozens of Native American organizations have officially condemned the team name for being racist. In the words of the Navajo professional golfer Notah Begay, the name is "a very clear example of institutionalized degradation of an ethnic minority" (Steinberg 2013). While many non–Native Americans, including the heads of the football team, argue that the name is all in good fun and there's nothing harmful about it, Begay disagrees: "I mean, if you look further and deeper into the issue, it's about the culture, it's about the identity, it's about the history of our people." Viewing the controversy from this perspective, Begay says, "if I were to take my kids to a Redskins game, and we were to see a non-native dressed up in traditional regalia, with eagle feathers in a headdress, dancing around, basically mocking the culture and the tradition, it would be very difficult to explain to my children."

Of course, not everyone with the same standpoint sees things the same way. Defenders of the Redskins' name point out that some Native Americans have no problem with it. And there are non–Native Americans who think the name should be changed. In other words, taking the power of **standpoint** seriously does not mean assuming that our ideas are mechanically determined by our identity and experience. Yet Begay makes an important observation about the power of standpoint when he suggests that the name Redskins tends to look different depending on whether it is viewed from the perspective of people whose cultures and traditions have long been attacked by the dominant culture in North America or from the perspective of the dominant culture itself. It is not impossible for people from different backgrounds "to achieve" or at least approach or appreciate the standpoint of others, but, as Hartsock says, doing so takes serious, ongoing work: genuine listening, a willingness to examine taken-for-granted assumptions critically, the recognition of unequal power relations, and more.

DECOLONIZING KNOWLEDGE

T HE HISTORY of Canada, the United States, Israel, and many other countries built by settlers on land that was already home to vibrant communities has been about not only the murder and displacement of individuals and groups but also the attempt to destroy the ways of knowing, the "standpoints," of the land's **Indigenous peoples**. Sir John A. Macdonald, the first prime minister of Canada, was very clear about this. In 1887, he said, "The great aim of our legislation," the *Indian Act*, which remains in force today, "has been to do away with the tribal system and assimilate the Indian people in all respects with the other inhabitants of the Dominion [of Canada] as speedily as they are fit to change" (quoted in Dickason 1992, 257). In addition to confiscating huge amounts of land, the Canadian government banned Indigenous languages and ceremonies and kidnapped aboriginal children, forcing them into government-run schools where they were beaten for speaking their own language, forced to dress and groom differently, educated in the official curriculum (which condemned

Indigenous identities), and often physically and sexually abused. The goal was to destroy culture, which can only survive over time by being passed between generations.

Many Indigenous writers contrast their ways of knowing the world with those associated with colonizing societies. For example, Vanessa Watts (2013, 22) writes that "as an Anishnaabe and Haudenosaunee woman, my worldview is continuously tested against the colonial frame." Watts uses the term "place-thought" to describe the basis of her way of knowing. "Place-thought is based upon the premise that land is alive and thinking" and that thoughts and actions are inseparable from relationships with the land. George Dei (2012, 112), writing about indigeneity in the African context, makes a similar point: "Indigenous cultural knowledge is about searching for wholeness and completeness," which means refusing to separate spirituality from knowledge (in the tradition of Western science), because "Spiritual identity is connected to the Land/Mother Earth and to one's inner self/soul and their physical and social surroundings."

These writers share concerns about the ways in which colonialism has destroyed Indigenous peoples' traditional relationships to the land, which are inseparable from their traditional ways of knowing. They emphasize wholeness and challenge the distinctions that tend to characterize colonizing perspectives, for example, between spiritual and rational or between human and non-human. Yet it would be wrong to suggest that they are proposing a single, coherent "Indigenous Knowledge," which stands opposed to "Western Knowledge" as the one right way of thinking. Indigenous peoples in different parts of the world are guided by different experiences, knowledge traditions, and spiritual understandings, and each group learns and practices knowledge differently.

What's more, the Ghanaian political theorist Ato Sekyi-Out (1996) argues that the history of colonialism has involved a two-way movement of knowledge between colonizer and colonized. Of course, he is clear that this has by no means been a free and equitable exchange of ideas. Nevertheless, he says, centuries of social interaction does make it difficult to divide Indigenous and Western knowledge into neat, isolated categories, each capable of being preserved and practiced in pure, untouched form. Knowledge traditions have informed each other. Consider the fact that Frantz Fanon was a revolutionary thinker and activist fighting against European colonialism, but his work was deeply informed by Karl Marx, Sigmund Freud, and other European thinkers. Pam Palmater (2013) is a lawyer and a professor at a major Canadian university, but she was also instrumental in launching the 2012 Idle No More movement for Indigenous sovereignty against what she calls the "assimilation agenda" of the Canadian government.

This book focuses on the foundations of methodical inquiry as they have been developed in Western social sciences. Indigenous ways of knowing the world, such as the ones discussed by Watts and Dei, challenge the very basis of social science approaches. For example, as the following chapters explain, methodical social science inquiry is based on clear distinction between facts, on the one hand, and stories on the other. Further, **social science** involves abstract concepts that generalize in ways very distant from personal experience and from any connection to a particular location. This abstract thinking is in tension with Watts's emphasis on knowledge as being "not distinct from place," as well as with the central role of storytelling in many Indigenous traditions.

Although the main focus of this book is not Indigenous ways of knowing or the rich debates surrounding them, we raise the discussion here and return to it at various points for two main reasons. First, Indigenous perspectives raise important questions about the limits of social science as a way of knowing. Western humanities and social sciences generally present themselves as the best ways of knowing the human condition, yet they are based on the experiences of some people while excluding the perspectives of others. For example, Western ways of knowing tend to privilege written sources above any others. However, Jeff Corntassel, Chawwin-is, and T'lakwadzi (2009, 137) argue that "storytelling is connected to our homelands and is crucial to the cultural and political resurgence of Indigenous nations." They suggest that attempts to forge new relations between Indigenous and settler societies must value storytelling just as much as the written sources and institutions dominant in the West, such as government research, parliamentary procedure, and private property. Indigenous conceptions of the interdependence among land, humans, non-human life, dreams, and the spirit world blow open the tendency within social science to separate the world into isolated fields of study—and to leave out the question of spiritual forces altogether. We think it's important to reflect on the advantages and limits of both social science and Indigenous approaches when developing frameworks for knowing the human condition. The chart comparing Indigenous and social science ways of knowing identifies several core characteristics of each. It is not included to suggest that these approaches stand in a simple black-and-white relationship of difference. The purpose of the chart is to help you recognize core themes in ongoing debates over different ways of knowing, so you can decide for yourself how varying perspectives relate to each other.

Second, addressing tensions between Indigenous perspectives and Western social science must be part of broader processes of genuine decolonization. It will ultimately be up to you to decide whether the sorts of theoretical thinking introduced in this book can be a force for liberation or whether they are inherently colonizing and oppressive. Following Lewis Gordon and Jane Gordon (2005), we think it is possible to draw on the best of different knowledge traditions in struggling for truth and a decolonized, democratic, free and fair world for all. In any case, being committed to decolonization means understanding the deep tensions between dominant and marginalized ways of understanding reality, so, at various points in the book, we raise questions about the relationship between social science, colonialism, and decolonization, and note how Indigenous ways of knowing help to reveal the limits of social science, a Western perspective that many scholars simply take for granted as the basis for reliable knowledge.

Core Characteristics of Indigenous Knowledge as a Way of Knowing the World	Core Characteristics of Social Science as a Way of Knowing the World
Aims to guide harmonious living among people, plants and animals, and the spirit world	Aims to generate trustworthy, generalizable knowledge about the human condition based on the combination of rigorous observation and the use of formal social theory
Emphasizes the importance of traditional knowledge passed down through storytelling and ceremonies, as well as written documents	Emphasizes the importance of written research and theory that has been scrutinized by experts in the field under study
Views spirituality as an integral part of understanding and acting on the world	Views spirituality as individual beliefs, which researchers must set aside during inquiry so as not to influence the research process
Does not distinguish sharply between human life, the natural environment, and the spirit world	Guided by strong categorical distinctions between nature, culture, and spirituality
Conducted every day on an ongoing basis to inform personal and group action by all members of a particular community	Most often conducted by specialists within academic, government, and commercial institutions with the aim of publishing results, informing public policy, or achieving business success
Has played an important role in resisting Western colonialism (although, there have at times been conflicts among different Indigenous groups)	Has played an important role in the Western colonization of Indigenous peoples (although some traditions within social science have criticized this role)

THINKING THEORETICALLY IN ORDER TO SOLVE PROBLEMS

THEORY CAN seem like a distraction to people who want to solve problems. "We know what the problem is," they say. "Let's stop wasting time talking and actually *do* something about it." It's easy to sympathize with this point of view, especially considering the overwhelming problems we face at the start of the twenty-first century: climate change, poverty, war, discrimination, and more. Climate change experts say that without massive adjustments in our relationship to the environment soon human life as we know it will be destroyed. We don't have decades to theorize what's going on before acting differently.

The problem with the "Let's get on with it!" approach is that it ignores the ways in which the best theoretical thinking is never fully separate from action. In fact, theory and action always inform each other, whether it's obvious or not.

Imagine you walk into a shoe store to find the clerk lying on the floor. Surely this is a time for action if there ever was one. But act how? Perhaps you decide to call 911 because the clerk's unresponsiveness tells you he's not just napping. Already you're being guided by a conceptual framework about how to determine a medical emergency and what to do should you find yourself in one. If you've had some first-aid training, you'd likely check to see if the clerk's airways are blocked or start doing CPR. Again, in the immediate context of the situation, this response can feel like "just acting," but not only are your actions informed by prior knowledge, they're also being shaped by what you're learning moment by moment in the situation. The constant back and forth between your core assumptions about what's going on and the experience of acting to help the fallen clerk is happening so fast you don't even notice. When the medical team arrives, they bring a new level of theoretical knowledge—richer frameworks for assessing the problem and acting on it. Of course, they too are likely to have their original frameworks reshaped as a result of what they do in the shoe store, which may end up strengthening their approach to similar situations in the future.

Yes, climate change is an urgent problem. But can it be reversed by everyone recycling and using more energy efficient light bulbs, or does our entire economy need to be transformed? "Let's get on with it," sure; but get on with what, exactly? Simply acting, in the absence of guiding frameworks for action, risks not helping at best and perhaps even making the situation worse. We need clear definitions of problems (which will, of course, be informed by prior action) and clear strategies for addressing them (which will, of course, be shaped by the experience of acting). Providing these definitions and strategies is the role of theory in problem solving.

Yet it's not only these big global problems that require theoretical thinking if they're to be solved. Your own problems, both inside and outside the classroom, are likely to become more manageable if they are more systematically approached using a process of inquiry grounded in theoretical thinking. For example, imagine you've been assigned to write an essay that examines whether "millennials"—people born since the mid-1980s—are as lazy and selfish as they are depicted to be in movies, newspapers, and by most profs. You probably already have a view about this, based on generalizations from your own experiences. You may know that your roommates skip class more often than they attend it or that your boss at the grocery store is always complaining about how much food gets stolen by students. Theoretical thinking can help connect these generalizations from experience to your research essay in a variety of ways.

For one thing, thinking theoretically involves questioning whether we have the right facts in the first place. There may be evidence of widespread laziness and selfishness at hand, but surely there is evidence of the opposite trend too. Lots of students skip class so they can attend band practice, do paid work, or exercise. Thinking theoretically involves reflecting on the basic terms we are using and how they frame the question. For example, how are we defining the term "lazy" when it comes to making generalizations about young people? Theoretical thinking also pushes us to seek explanations for social patterns when they are observed, rather than simply assuming their meaning is clear. Do students skip class because they're lazy or because classes are boring and unlikely to promote learning, given that they are jammed with hundreds of students and a prof at the front who drones on for three hours straight? Do people steal because they're selfish or because wages have failed to keep up with rising prices, forcing more and more people into poverty? These aren't simply questions of fact. They require explanation, and that involves theoretical thinking. The next chapter moves the conversation from thinking theoretically in a general sense to three of the main traditions of formal theoretical thinking within academic research.

2

Theory Matters

Even after reading the first chapter of this book, you may still wonder if theory really speaks to you. It might seem obvious that you would learn more by piling up a supply of solid facts than by studying laborious theoretical explanations based on abstract claims about human nature and social justice. Actually, theory can seem to be the enemy of fact, undercutting observation by introducing what appears to be bias from the outset.

It is a widespread assumption that the best knowledge comes from systematic observations, allowing for the accumulation of data. People, however, cannot simply record sense data neutrally. Observation always involves choices. Think about it: every time you enter a room, you focus your attention. It is impossible to capture everything, so any act of observation is necessarily one of framing and selecting. Simply reading this book involves ignoring a lot of other sensations competing for your attention. Or maybe you are not ignoring them? This theme is covered in much more detail in Chapter 5.

As we move from observation to explanation, we draw on what we already know about the phenomena we are investigating to understand why things happen as they do. People do this theorizing all the time, often without even thinking about it. You hear a sudden loud noise and assume it is a vehicle backfire, fireworks, or a gunshot depending on your own previous experiences and understanding of the context.

The rigorous process of investigation associated with social science and humanities disciplines pushes us to be much more methodical about the ways we observe and explain. Your Grandma is a wonderful source of knowledge and a great source of wisdom, but her understanding of biology may be quite limited. As a child, it was fine to believe her story that the first horse was born out of the secret love affair between a donkey and a unicorn, but unquestioned acceptance of this story now will not get you good marks on your next exam about evolution. Scholarly disciplines are based on a process of critical investigation, in which you must evaluate the sources of your knowledge and reflect on your own position in the process of observation.

Further, these disciplines are committed to drawing on what people already know when we analyse phenomena. Generally, people are remarkably good improvisational explainers, drawing very quickly on the storehouse of fact and opinion that sits in their brains to seek an understanding of something they see, hear, feel, taste, or touch. This ingenuity can lead to a lot of reinventing the wheel, as improvisers seek to work out for themselves something that is already well known to experts. You may have figured out, for example, that grapefruit juice is a magical hangover cure, but you would not have needed all that experimentation if you simply found the existing scientific research that clarifies the role of dehydration in suffering the day after drinking. Drinking pretty much any non-alcoholic liquid will help. Your grapefruit cure may convince pals in a bar argument but will not be persuasive in a more formal setting.

In the context of scholarly disciplines, explanations are rooted in and developed through the use of formal theories. Each formal theory is a link to a vast repository of established knowledge. Of course, formal theories do not always already hold the answers to all our questions. The problems and issues scholars study will have their own unique character that requires careful investigation. Formal theories guide and inform the process of study and observation, helping to define what the problems are in the first place and how they might be addressed. Using these formal theories means making deliberate choices about framing our knowledge, both at the level of how we do the research (method) and how we develop explanations (theory).

In this section, we will discuss the ways formal theories are based on a few founding assumptions, or central premises. The universe of formal theory is comprised of different schools of thought, each one sharing a set of common premises. These shared premises answer fundamental questions; here are just a few: Is this a just world? How did things get to be this way? What can we expect in the future? How do we know?

The most effective way to engage with formal theories is to develop an understanding of the key premises of each school. This map of foundational ideas allows you to trace back the logic that links the analysis of a particular issue, such as crime, to a core of assumptions about the way the world works. We will introduce this concept by looking at one crucial debate that has influenced theoretical analysis in the social sciences: social order versus conflict. We are not claiming that this debate is the single key to opening every lock down the corridors of theory. Rather, it is one debate that has the advantage of clearly polarized positions, a long history of disputation, and fairly obvious application to a variety of contemporary social and political issues.

Theories based on the **social order model** make certain assumptions about the way the world works and how things change. The **conflict model** disputes pretty much every one of those assumptions. **Postmodern approaches** reject both social order and conflict models, arguing that they issue from the same faulty system of knowledge. Tracking down the central premises of a theory will provide you with an interpretive edge as you begin to make sense of the particular features and details. Trying to learn a theory as a set of facts is much more difficult and less rewarding than seeking to understand it in the light of its key founding assumptions.

SOCIAL ORDER: THE BATTLE
AGAINST CHAOS

THE CENTRAL premise of the social order model is that society is the crucial regulator that keeps people from acting in their narrow self-interest without the slightest regard for others. Lurking just beneath the surface of our socialized selves are brutal self-serving beasts that will seize whatever they desire to satisfy their wants and needs. Society restrains the beasts and thus makes order possible.

The social order model underlies the work of many theorists, including Thomas Hobbes, Auguste Comte, Émile Durkheim, Talcott Parsons, and W.W. Rostow. It is the cornerstone of the functionalist school of social thought, the dominant perspective in sociology and in many of the social sciences until the 1960s. The Canadian sociologist Frank Pearce (2001) makes a strong argument that Durkheim was a much more radical thinker than the typical social order theorist, but the main reason that Pearce wrote his book in the first place is that most scholars have interpreted Durkheim's work as a classic formulation of **functionalism**, where we seek explanations for phenomena in terms of how they contribute to the operation of society as a whole. Functionalism is still highly influential in academic disciplines and in politics; you are likely to find echoes of some of the positions articulated by conservative politicians in contemporary debates as you examine this model.

The social order model presumes that a well-regulated society serves the interests of all by protecting us against the threat of savagery that lies within us and throughout humankind. William Golding's novel *Lord of the Flies* (1958) provides an interesting illustration of this perspective. A group of children stranded on a desert island start their stay by trying to preserve civilization but end up going wild. Early on, they try to establish an orderly regime. In the words of Jack, "We've got to have rules and obey them. After all, we're not savages. We're English; and the English are best at everything. So we've got to do the right things" (Golding 1958, 47). By the end, they have become a terrifying mob the narrator refers to as "the tribe." In one incident, they chase after Ralph, the deposed leader: "Ralph stumbled, feeling not pain but panic, and the tribe, screaming now like the Chief, began to advance. . . . Ralph turned and ran. A great noise as of seagulls rose behind him" (Golding 1958, 200–01). If you have ever heard a flock of screeching gulls, you can imagine the sounds Ralph heard as he fled from the mob.

We will come back to this novel in Chapter 6, and there we will address the ethnocentrism connected to the images of British civilization pitted against brutal savagery. It is ethnocentric to assume your own **culture** is superior to others and therefore to judge others as lesser.

Lord of the Flies serves as a vivid illustration of the idea that social order is a particular product of societal regulation that protects us from the descent into chaos and bloodshed. The social order model seeks to develop social theory as a tool to help us understand how order is possible in the face of the constant threat of degeneration into self-serving brutality. The second premise that follows from this core assumption is that a population with a strong set of shared norms and values is one of the most important elements in maintaining an orderly society. People who share a common set of norms and values require a minimum of external policing to keep them in line as they have internalized the habit of regulating themselves.

It might seem that these common values would be threatened by social stratification, the division of society into a hierarchy in which some people have much more power and access to resources than do others. Stratification can create unrest if people at the lower end of the scale feel unjustly exploited. However, advocates of the social order model argue that people will accept social hierarchy providing that they see the system is fair and feel that their own contribution to the work of society is properly recognized. Indeed, stratification can be the basis for an efficient division of labour and a source of motivation for hard work as people seek advancement. The motivational effects of stratification become particularly important in large-scale, complex industrial societies where the division of labour is highly specialized, so jobs are highly differentiated from one another.

It follows, then, that advocates of the social order model argue that the role of the state is to preserve social order within a particular territory by enforcing these norms, whether by punishing wrongdoers or by socializing the population so that it internalizes society's values. In an industrial society, this role pushes the state towards pluralism in the political process, meaning that competing interest groups (such as employers' organizations, trade unions, farmers' groups, ethnic and cultural associations, women's organizations, etc.)

are represented. Negotiation between interest groups tends to produce acceptable outcomes over time, providing that no one is unfairly excluded from the process.

Consequently, advocates of this social order model can and do advocate social change, if it is required to eliminate unjust practices that serve as obstacles to pluralist participation in the production of a societal consensus based on shared values. Indeed, it is the character of modern industrial society that those who wish to preserve social order must, at times, call for social change to handle the economic, technological, and cultural innovation produced by this kind of society. A pluralist state is particularly important for helping society through this process of change in an orderly manner. The reconciliation of order and change is one of the marks of this social order model.

Finally, it follows from the core assumptions of the social order model that the spread of industrial society to the less developed areas of the world should be understood as a process of modernization that benefits everyone. The contemporary process of globalization, as understood by this model, is simply the latest stage in a long-term modernization process. The gap between richer and poorer nations is explained in this perspective in terms of success or failure at launching into the development of a thriving industrial society. Those nations that succeed in the development of a modern industrial society thrive, while others fail to prosper.

CONFLICT: CHALLENGING INEQUITIES

THE CONFLICT model rejects the assumption that the preservation of social order serves us all by protecting against the threat of chaos. Instead, its basic premise is that our present society is organized around fundamental inequalities that can be overcome only by a substantial transformation of social relations. The core assumption of this model is that social inequality produces conflict that leads to change. The disadvantaged have their own interests that conflict with those who occupy the key power positions in society. As they begin to act on the basis of these interests, those in subordinate positions have the capacity to challenge the existing social order and change the world. This transformation happens, for example, when workers organize into unions; people of colour challenge racism; women build movements for reproductive freedom, equity at work, and against violence; or lesbians and gay men fight back against heterosexism.

The conflict model is the foundation for many strands of Marxist, **feminist**, anti-racist, and lesbian-gay liberationist theories. In this view, society does not civilize people through moral regulation but rather stymies the human development of the disadvantaged through oppression rooted in systemic inequalities. Disadvantaged people are denied the chance to meet their full human potential and are therefore stunted by the experience of exploitation and oppression. The conflict model does not simply express compassion for the disadvantaged as victims of the system but views them as social actors with the potential to change the world.

In the conflict model, theory is a tool to help unleash human capacities by challenging the power structure that keeps people down. George Orwell (1966, 8–9) offers a vision of this kind of liberation in his vivid description of revolutionary Barcelona in 1936:

> It was the first time I had ever been in a town where the working class was in the saddle. . . . Waiters and shopwalkers looked you in the eye and treated you as an equal. Servile and even ceremonial styles of speech had disappeared. Nobody said "*Señor*" or "*Don*" or even "*Usted*"; everyone called everyone else "Comrade" and "Thou," and said "*Salud!*" instead of "*Buenos días.*" Tipping was forbidden by law. . . . There were no private motor cars, they had all been commandeered. . . . The revolutionary posters were everywhere, flaming from the walls in clean reds and blues. . . . In outward appearance it was a town in which the wealthy classes had practically ceased to exist. . . . Practically everyone

wore rough working-class clothes, or blue overalls, or some variant of the militia uniform. All this was queer and moving. There was much in it I did not understand, in some ways I did not even like it, but I recognized it immediately as a state of affairs worth fighting for.

The transformation of **power relations** Orwell described was so thoroughgoing that it produced new ways of acting towards each other, including more direct eye contact and the elimination of the old deferential and formal ways of addressing those more powerful than yourself, like "sir" or "ma'am" or "professor." These are signs of the development of new forms of **consciousness** and new ways of living as the disadvantaged stake their claims for a more just world.

The conflict model is therefore critical of the idea of shared norms and values based on inequality in the present society. Rather than a genuine consensus, these are seen as ideologies that support the ruling order and perpetuate the disadvantaged status of the subordinate groups. For example, the American dream of rising from rags to riches might disguise the reality that most people move very little from the social position of their parents and that most of the powerful started life in advantaged positions.

The state, in this conflict model, does not serve the interests of all by defending social order against chaos but rather acts on behalf of the most powerful by protecting a particular inequitable order against the claims of the disadvantaged. The state might appear to be a neutral referee as contending interest groups stake their claims on a level playing field, but, according to the conflict model, the rules of the game favour the powerful every time. The representation of subordinate groups within the corridors of power might create the illusion of full participation but generally does not result in a significant change in the condition of the bulk of the disadvantaged population.

Social inequality amounts to exploitation, according to the conflict model. Privileges and resources flow to those in positions of power, while the contribution of the disadvantaged is always undervalued. The powerful might try to present this

Key Contrasts between Social Order and Conflict Theories

Theoretical Perspective	Assumptions about Society	Assumptions about Dominant Values	Assumptions about Social Inequality	Assumptions about Social Change	Assumptions about Theory
Social Order Theory	Society is the crucial regulator that prevents people from acting in their narrow self-interest, and makes it possible for large groups of people to live relatively peaceful and productive lives.	Social order is maintained by a strong set of shared norms and values, as well as a strong state. A healthy society will promote shared values and a common culture.	People will accept inequality provided that they believe that the overall system is fair and that people at the low end of society have the chance to move up the ranks if they work hard.	Change is sometimes necessary in order to eliminate unjust practices that threaten continued order and stability. Meaningful social change can be imposed from above.	Theory should be developed as a tool to help us understand how to maintain order.
Conflict Theory	Society is not free, fair, and based on equality for all; rather, society is organized around fundamental inequalities that privilege some groups and individuals and disadvantage others.	Dominant norms and values, as well as the powers of the state, effectively support the ruling order and marginalize subordinate groups. A common culture hides these realities.	Inequality plays a central role in shaping modern societies. The privilege of certain groups is maintained through the exploitation of other groups.	Substantive social change occurs when subordinate groups actively challenge the existing social order and construct new forms of social relations. Meaningful social change must come from below.	Theory is a tool to help unleash human capacities by challenging the power structure that keeps disadvantaged groups down.

arrangement as a legitimate system in which those who have the most abilities rise to the top and provide the leadership we all require, but, from the perspective of the conflict model, the resources and privileges of the powerful can have only one source—the exploitation of the disadvantaged.

Inequality amounts to exploitation on a global scale, as well. The so-called Third World is not simply slower to take off into wonderful modernization but has been intentionally underdeveloped by the actions of the dominant nations, both in the period of colonization and since national independence. The dominant nations and the transnational corporations associated with them maintain their power in the global system through economic, political, and military activities.

POSTMODERNISM: CHALLENGING
THOUGHT SYSTEMS

POSTMODERN PERSPECTIVES dismiss both the social order and conflict models discussed above, arguing that they share the same flawed foundations. Although the social order and conflict approaches may seem to be polar opposites engaged in pitched debate, postmodernist critics argue that these thought systems have more in common than it seems at first glance. Social order and conflict theories both share key premises associated with modernist outlooks that postmodernist approaches reject.

According to the *OED Online* (2014), modern means "Characteristic of the present time, or the time of writing; not old-fashioned, antiquated, or obsolete." Modernism means "sympathy with or affinity for what is modern." The idea of post (meaning after) modern at first seems contradictory, suggesting a move beyond "the present time." However, in the history of political and cultural ideas, the notion of "modernism" as advocating for the current rather than the obsolete is not used in an abstract, timeless way. It refers to a very specific time and place: namely, the modern era, rooted in Europe. This era began with a wave of uprisings when the old order was overthrown and replaced by new ways of thinking and of organizing society.

The French Revolution (1789–99) is a pivotal event that is often used to mark the beginning of the modern era in Europe. The king was beheaded and the nobility lost its stranglehold on the operation of the economy. New ideas of freedom and equality entered into political discussion and debate. The role of the Catholic Church as the only legal religion was abolished, and the state was established as a secular realm, not associated with any specific creed. At the same time, the slaves of Haiti, France's most profitable colony, rose up to demand their own freedom.

The French Revolution is seen as the moment when Enlightenment thinking moved from marginal and persecuted status to become the dominant intellectual framework. Enlightenment thought emphasized rationality and scientific inquiry, casting doubt on traditional ways of knowing based on faith and the role of supernatural forces. At the most basic level, Enlightenment thinking is associated with the idea that everything is ultimately knowable if we simply develop the right ways of finding out. This ongoing expansion of our knowledge base, as we develop better methods and probe deeper into the universe around us, will provide us with the ability to make progress in challenging the world's problems.

Postmodernist thinkers argue that both social order and conflict theories derive from the Enlightenment ideas that marked **modernity**. Though postmodernist thinkers are a highly diverse bunch, with very different perspectives on many debates, they tend to share a fundamental critique of modernist social theories focused on three key points.

First, though the core ideas of Enlightenment thinking claim to be universal, encompassing all of humanity in a vision of a better future, modernity, in fact, reflects a very specific European male perspective grounded in particular historical experiences. The audacity, for example, to claim a single mode of thought as "the" Enlightenment (in the singular) reflects the limits of this project. Modernity erases the experiences, the perspectives, and the agency of women, and Indigenous and racialized people, reducing history to a simple hypocritical story of progress radiating out from Europe through the activity of colonizing powers. Indeed, modernist thought constructs the brutal spread of European conquest and economic exploitation as a kind of secular salvation accomplished through modernization and development in place of the moral salvation of the old missionaries. This supposed elevation of the "uncivilized" was hypocritical, as those who were colonized were never treated as fully human by their conquerors. "The European colonizer both preached this Enlightenment humanism at the colonized and at the same time denied it in practice" (Chakrabarty 2000, 4).

Second, modernity notably failed to deliver the goods in practice. Neither social order nor conflict theories have, according to the postmodern perspective, produced a genuine improvement in human life. In the name of modernist conceptions of liberty and equality, people have created new forms of domination and subordination ranging from Soviet-style bureaucratic communism through liberal democracy to fascism. This track record does not inspire postmodernists, who tend to argue that grand experiments in social transformation end up producing new forms of injustice.

Third, postmodernists argue that the basic approach to knowledge underlying Enlightenment thinking is deeply flawed. The tools of inquiry we develop to understand the world do not, in any simple way, offer up better knowledge. In fact, they offer distorted versions of the world that merely reflect pre-existing framing assumptions. These assumptions, which empower some and not others, are disguised in the eventual knowledge claims, made to appear as though they emerged from research. Science, for example, says the postmodernist, cannot produce an objective model of what exists but always includes subjective choices about everything from measurement to interpretation.

Key Contrasts between Modernism and Postmodernism

	Modernism (social order and conflict theories)	Postmodernism
Scope	Orientation towards the universal, understanding the world in terms of general laws that apply to all of humanity	Orientation towards the particular, as universal rules for humanity tend to be based on generalizations from specific experiences
Knowledge	Enlightenment model in which humans gain ever-greater knowledge as they develop capacities to probe the mysteries of life; this ever-improving knowledge base creates possibilities for progress—in medicine, technology, governance, and other areas	Human knowledge is limited; inquiry is always framed by existing categories shaped by dominant power relations, so the goal of serious analysis is to critique existing knowledge, laying bare its presuppositions
Role of theory in relation to social change	Science contributes to social change by revealing the social dynamics that allow people to regulate their futures, either protecting the world from the threat of disorder or overcoming inequalities	Rejection of deliberate projects of change in which people develop blueprints for a better world and try to implement them, arguing these tend to produce totalitarianism

THEORETICAL PLURALISM

In the humanities and social sciences, formal theorizing tends to be an area of vibrant debate. It should be obvious from the three frameworks sketched above that a social order theorist, a conflict theorist, and a postmodernist could look at the same set of facts and come to very different conclusions. Their contrasting interpretations would not necessarily be caused by disagreement about the basic facts; rather, disputes would be rooted in the clash of fundamental premises about how people know and what justice looks like. Of course, holding such different fundamental assumptions means they would likely even dispute the facts themselves, asking in various ways whether we can know in objective ways, as is discussed in Chapter 3.

Part of learning to think through scholarly disciplines is making sense of this **theoretical pluralism**. For some people, this understanding may take the form of a strong orientation towards one model, for example social order, conflict, or postmodernism, in the comparative framework. You might actually begin to recognize some of your own core beliefs about the world reflected back through the more rigorous frame of formal theory. Even if you strongly align with a particular theory, however, you cannot simply casually dismiss the others. You will learn more through engaging with them deeply and understanding how particular conclusions derive from specific premises.

On the other hand, you may not feel an attachment to any of these theoretical models. They may seem like a lot of bloated ivory tower bafflegab from your perspective; or your own fundamental beliefs may lie outside this comparative matrix. You can still hone your thinking skills by engaging seriously with formal theories and the debates that result from theoretical pluralism. The more you recognize the way fundamental premises frame processes of inquiry in a way that leads to specific conclusions, the more you can be persuasive in supporting or debunking arguments and positions.

In the previous chapter, the distinction was drawn between theory, fact, and opinion. Without recognizing it, we often rely on opinion alone to make arguments. Just look, for example, at the reviews people post on social media about movies, music, television shows, or restaurants: loved it, hated it, tasted great, puke. If you compare these reviews to those of highly skilled critics, you recognize a real difference. The skilled critic will tell you something about the craft of the actors, the way the director handled the pacing of the story, or name the specific ingredient that overwhelmed the flavour of the dish. You will learn things you did not already know and develop skills to reflect more deeply about your own reaction to particular shows, art pieces, or dishes.

Of course, even if you ultimately understand all the craft brought to the table by a particular chef cooking a specific dish, it still might not be to your liking. There is plenty of room for dispute and debate, for example, about the role of music in telling a good story in film. But you will be able to enter into the discussion at a whole different level, with much more persuasive power, because you have analysed the process and understood how the final results were developed.

Engagement with formal theories trains your mind to understand the process of the development of ideas, linking observation through analysis to the construction of conclusions. This knowledge will help make you a better researcher, whether in the formal sense of writing university papers or in the everyday sense of accumulating information about a job before an interview so you can figure out how to answer questions effectively in that context. Further, you will recognize that theoretical pluralism focuses our attention squarely on fundamental disputes that often lie beneath the surface of our arguments, for example about human nature, the way we know, and what a better world might look like.

Thinking Point: Five-Star Critics

As a group, discuss this question: "What might persuade us to buy a concert ticket to see performers we did not already know?" Would it be an online review or a review in an established publication or the assessment of a friend expressed in conversation? Discuss the strengths and weaknesses of these different critical venues. As a follow-up, find an example of an online review and one from an established publication and assess the differences between them.

TROUBLED TIMES, IN THEORY

To GET a better sense of theoretical pluralism, we just need to look to debates in the world around us. To repeat one of the central themes of this book, theory is not something that exists only in the specialized and often distant world of academic debate. On the contrary, theory is all around us. Whenever we encounter people seriously disagreeing over the nature, causes, and consequences of social issues, very likely part of what is making it so hard for them to agree is that they are approaching the same issue from different theoretical positions.

For example, hardly anyone would dispute the fact that in 2008–09, the world was in the midst of the worst economic crisis since the end of World War II. Over eight months, the stock market fell dramatically and several big banks and corporations totally collapsed. The future of many other businesses looked bleak. The unemployment rate rose continuously, leaving millions of working people without money to pay their bills and feed their families. Unions in various countries went on strike in order to protect themselves from the labour restructuring proposed by cash-strapped governments.

In times such as these, not even the most optimistic observer would deny that the global economic system was in major trouble and that billions of people suffered as a result. In fact, in October 2008, Alan Greenspan, the former head of the US Federal Reserve and long-time capitalist cheerleader, admitted to a committee of US senators that "we are in the midst of a once-in-a-century credit tsunami." However, although it was widely understood that the world was in a very dangerous place, there was disagreement over exactly what caused the crisis, how it would play out, and how it could be ended. It is within disagreements such as this that elements of social order and conflict theory can be spotted.

Consider two popular ways of understanding the roots of the crisis. On the one hand, by comparing the crisis to a "tsunami," Greenspan and others who share his view suggest that large-scale breakdowns in the global economy are natural parts of life. This view is consistent with the social order perspective, which believes that unforeseen calamities and sudden hardships are unavoidable features of large-scale societies. The fact that the system broke down is an indication that the regulations meant to protect against this sort of disaster were obviously not stringent enough. The actions of greedy CEOs, reckless financial advisors, and short-sighted consumers caused this unprecedented collapse by exploiting weaknesses in the system in pursuit of personal advantage.

On the other hand, people who view the crisis from the perspective of conflict theory argue that the breakdown in the global economy was not merely a part of the natural cycle of growth and decline, and they reject the notion that the crisis was caused by reckless or greedy individuals. By contrast, from this perspective, the crisis is viewed as the more-or-less predictable outcome of the inequalities and instability built into the core of Western societies. The reigning global economic system makes it easy for multinational banks and corporations to avoid government oversight, encourages corporations and individuals to take huge risks with their money, perpetuates both the overproduction and overconsumption of goods (which, in turn, places great strains on the natural environment), and fails to ensure that all people are provided with adequate social services and standards of living. The bulk of people around the world live in a constant state of crisis; how could this *not* lead to a total breakdown in the system?

Let us now turn our attention from different ways of understanding the causes of the crisis to varying interpretations of the trillions of public dollars given to ailing private companies—that is, the so-called government bailouts. As suggested already, the social order perspective fears a loss of social stability more than anything. The thinking behind this fear is that shakiness in one area of society is likely to spread to others and could end up triggering an even more devastating collapse of the whole social system. It was the social order perspective, therefore, that drove politicians and economists to support billions of government dollars being given to the General Motors car company *despite* its poor business record and bloated corporate structure. Fearing that its failure would ripple through other sectors of the economy, backers of the bailout explained that the company was simply "too big to fail." Bailouts were certainly unpalatable to many of the politicians who voted in favour of them; however, they were deemed necessary to protect specific major firms and to maintain the integrity of the overall socioeconomic system.

Although the conflict perspective is critical of government bailouts, it is unlikely to reject them altogether. After all, the failure of General Motors would hurt not only "fat-cat" executives but thousands of hard-working labourers and their families. Even people with radical left politics, people who tend to be informed by conflict theory, might support government bailouts because they don't want to see working people devastated by unemployment. Nevertheless, unlike the perspectives that guide most politicians, bankers, economists, and other people in positions of authority, conflict theory helps to highlight questions about why governments were so quick to bail out banks and big business when these very same governments repeatedly dismiss calls to fund large-scale social programs such as national day care, universal health care, or a living wage for all. On the one hand, governments argue that we all have to tighten our belts in tough times and demand that striking workers accept concessions to their contracts; yet, on the other hand, governments shovel cash to floundering corporations as fast as the money can be printed. The contradiction supports a fundamental assumption of conflict theory, namely, that mainstream political institutions and cultural practices systematically favour dominant groups and individuals.

Virtually everyone wants the crisis to end, but, again, specific visions of the future depend a great deal upon a person's theoretical perspective. One dominant way of thinking—the one most closely aligned with social order theory—wants a return to economic stability and the economic expansion of the 1990s and early 2000s. It is true that even supporters of Western governments and free-market **capitalism** believe that new checks must be placed upon banks and businesses in order to protect against another crisis like this one. However, regardless of the extent to which such policies would revise current practices, their purpose would be to preserve the existing social order, not to create a radically different one.

Conversely, others point out the fact that even in so-called prosperous times, Western societies are both home to and the source of a whole range of different crises. The list is long and disheartening: poverty; homelessness; environmental degradation; war; the displacement of Indigenous peoples from their traditional lands; sexism, racism, and homophobia; more and more stress placed on working people and fewer and fewer opportunities for them to participate in democratic forms of government; disease and hunger in some places and outrageous decadence in others; and the ongoing impoverishment, alienation, and displacement of people in the Third World. What, the conflict theorist asks, is gained by a return to such an order? Who wins from the revitalization of "normal" social structures? Certainly not the people who were poor, unemployed, and oppressed even before the outbreak of the current crisis. The conflict theorist agrees that the crisis needs to end but argues that it must end in a way that does more than simply patch up the holes caused by the latest breakdown of an inherently flawed system. According to the perspective of conflict theory, society needs a fundamental change, and that change will not come from a new set of government policies from above but only through the struggles and democratic forms of organizing of those who are marginalized and oppressed by the system that led us into this crisis in the first place.

Postmodernists, in contrast, might point out how crises demonstrate the limits of human knowledge. Rather than seeking the definitive explanation of this crisis, postmodernists would tend to critique the dominant forms of knowledge being produced about this economic downturn. Economists, for example, take very specific measures as criteria to assess overall economic performance. These measures often obscure as much as they reveal, for example using growth as a central criterion for the health of the economy rather than the well-being of the population. Postmodernists would aim to reveal the ways economic measures not only reflect but also reinforce the dominant forms of power by hiding the real condition of the population and focusing on wealth-making as a supposedly neutral measure in the interests of all.

Comparing and contrasting very different theoretical approaches makes it easier to develop a general sense of what it means to think theoretically. By examining differences in the theoretical assumptions of strongly opposed views, we begin to detect patterns in theoretical thinking. Of course, the versions of social order, conflict, and postmodernist theories here are composites, labels intended to draw together major trends in social theory without claiming to account for every possible difference between specialized theoretical schools. The ability to trace an argument back to its core assumptions is extremely valuable in many contexts. The greatest debates in society tend not to be disputes over facts. After all, equipped with the proper instruments, we can determine easily enough whether the temperature of the ocean has increased or decreased over the past 30 years. These debates revolve around competing ways of interpreting and acting upon the facts, as people seek explanations for changes in ocean temperature and hash out responsibilities for action. The facts never speak for themselves, and learning to analyse an argument critically by tracing back the core premises underlying the interpretation being applied is a crucial skill.

FORMAL THEORIES VS. EVERYDAY THEORIZING

THE BASIS of theoretical thinking is to ask naïve questions about how things work in the environment around you. As we answer the simplest questions (particularly why and how as opposed to who, where, and when), we are pushed to investigate the causal processes that shape the world we inhabit. At some level, we all think theoretically when we speculate about the reasons things happen as they do. This reflection on the causes of things is absolutely essential as it is only when we can figure out what created a particular response at a specific moment that we can hope to repeat it with any predictability. Thus, each of us figures out our own vision of how things work through our daily lives. This task is important, and it serves us well. Our insights can gain still greater power, however, when they are related to those of others that have been formulated into more rigorous theories and tested over time. Our own insights are quite adequate to confirm that this glass will fall to the ground and shatter if James lets go of it. We will not, however, come to understand fully the workings of gravity on our own. We need access to the specialized thinking that has already developed in the area. And gaining access requires locating the role of theory within a cycle of inquiry that moves between empirical research and theoretical explanation.

The more formal theoretical thinking associated with the social sciences adds a new level of discipline to our everyday theorizing. Competitive athletes must move beyond their own natural abilities and intuitive responses through specialized training grounded in a broader understanding of the mechanics of the human body and the advanced techniques in their particular sport. We can similarly train ourselves to develop more rigorous insights and greater powers of persuasion through engaging with the best theoretical analysis that is available.

Everyday theorizing is comparable to pick-up hockey or home cooking; to get to another level requires new skills learned through a range of specialized exercises and a great deal of practice. These skills can be learned and, like athletics, some people probably have an easier time with them than others. Alan was always the worst in his class in gym, and knows that it was much more difficult for him to learn things that seemed second nature to others. James thrived on the dodge-ball court but failed math tests that classmates said were easy. You may feel this way about the study of theory. However, all of us have the potential to think theoretically, and developing this capacity can have an impact on our ability to act in the world.

Most of the time, we go through our lives simply accepting the world as it is. We do not seek explanations for the way things work. This attitude gets us through the day just fine, but it does hamper our ability to act in the world, to make changes. It is difficult to do very much about processes that seem to be shrouded in the cloak of mystery. Theoretical thinking can help us to pull back that cloak, moving from assuming that's just the way it is to asking why it is so. As we get to know the causes of things through methodical inquiry, we can begin doing something about them, whether that is understanding why some people get hired rather than others or figuring out why poverty persists in the midst of plenty in the contemporary world.

An engagement with formal theories is worthwhile when it takes us beyond our own individual, and at times eccentric, interpretations of the world to some sort of common framework for discussion and debate. You might develop a personal insight that television makes children violent on the basis of seeing some kids play at wrestling after watching a particular show. That personal insight might not be enough to persuade others, who might treat the incident as unusual and atypical. Your insight will have much more power if you relate it to existing debates on the subject as they are expressed through formal theories that meet rigorous criteria in such areas as logical consistency and fit with reality.

Five Characteristics of Formal Theorizing

1. Logical rigour
2. Empirical rigour
3. Conceptual rigour
4. Asks second-order questions
5. Relates to existing bodies of knowledge

There are five ways in which formal theorizing is more disciplined than everyday theoretical thinking.

1. *Logical rigour* provides a clear flow from the core assumptions of the theory to its detailed development. In everyday thinking, we are allowed more slack. If we hold two beliefs that do not fit together, the people we argue with—for instance, in a bar—are unlikely to hold us up to the strictest standards of logic by pointing out the contradictions. In bars, people often try to win arguments by being bombastic, loud, and cranky. This kind of argument often ends up with each person simply restating the same point again and again, barely listening to other points that might go against his or her own. We find that this kind of argument seldom moves us at all, as we are not challenged to reconsider the grounds of our own perspectives by some systematic thought.

A disciplined logical approach can be a kind of mental judo, using the force of your opponents' own arguments to topple them. The aim is to clarify the foundations for claims being made and to ensure the quality of the links in the chain connecting each point to the next. You might argue, for example, that dogs are smarter than cats because you can train them to do all kinds of things. A logical challenge to this point might ask whether it necessarily follows that obedience is a sign of intelligence. Might obedience not be a sign of stupidity as indicated by the lack of an independent will?

A good argument is disciplined by the standards of logical rigour. Formal theories are based on positions that flow logically from key premises. You can develop your own skills at logic through studying theory (as well as through specific logic courses). This will make you more persuasive as you gain the ability to detect the weak points in other people's arguments and to anticipate the flaws others might detect in your own.

2. Theoretical thinking calls for *empirical rigour*. This is one of the main points discussed in Chapter 3. Although a theory may fit with what we know about the world, the commitment to empirical rigour does not mean that every aspect of that theory is immediately testable with observation and measurement. Einstein, for example, developed innovative theoretical statements that could not be tested definitively at the time. There

are theories in physics that propose the existence of elements that are not visible even to the most sensitive instruments currently in use. We must ensure, however, that such a theory is supported by the evidence that we do have, and we must maintain the commitment to testing for indications that the theory fits the facts as we know them. In social theory we are always seeking some sort of match with the world out there.

Theoretical thinking without empirical investigation is speculation, the development of an explanation that *could* fit a particular case. Speculation can be extremely valuable, and it is an important feature of our everyday thinking. We often speculate about the causes of a particular phenomenon; for example, we try to figure out why a windshield wiper is not working well any more. The speculative explanation we come up with—the windshield and wiper blade are both dirty— might be adequate to meet our needs at the time, or it might not help. We will only know when we investigate further by trying the wipers after cleaning the windshield and blades.

More formal theory is based on a commitment to move beyond speculation into investigation. The fit between our explanation of the phenomenon and the actual flow of events is something that we can research. It is not enough to assert a connection between our speculative cause and the actual effect; we must do our best to demonstrate it. As discussed in Chapter 3, the exact type of investigation conducted depends on whether the researcher is working from a positivist, interpretive, or critical theory of knowledge.

On the other hand, empirical investigation without theoretical analysis is description, detailing the characteristics of the phenomenon without seeking an explanation. Journalism often tends to be descriptive rather than analytical. The news tells you what happened but does not often try to explain in any depth the reasons it happened. The supposed impartiality of journalism rests, in part, on the claim that it is the facts that get reported, though even so the facts are selected and arranged in ways that are far from neutral.

Social theory moves beyond description to analysis and asks challenging causal questions that cannot be answered at the level of the facts alone. If you follow the plot in any good detective novel, you will find the points at which the crime solver moves beyond the facts to analysis and theory. As a reader, it's easy to get stuck at the level of the facts of the case and fail to put the picture together with theoretical thinking to figure out who did it.

3. Formal theories operate with great *conceptual rigour*. It is a standard feature of everyday language use that we employ words we do not fully understand because we have heard them in a context and think we know what they mean. That usually works fine, though we have all probably been caught out at some time using a new word incorrectly. In rigorous theoretical work, the words are the tools of the craft, and you must treat them with special attention. It is good to make friends with a dictionary as you work through social theory and at times to supplement that with a specialist source associated with the particular discipline you are working within.

This conceptual rigour is also reflected in the use of a specialized vocabulary that might seem quite alien. You will encounter words that mess with your brain a little. Your first response might be to feel that you are being jerked around by someone who has spent too many years in school and is using big words to show off and intimidate you. We would not deny for a second that many academics could benefit from enhancing their communication skills. But it is also true that specialized concepts can be developed as highly refined tools to work with great precision on the analysis of our social relations. For example, there are no simple everyday words to capture the meaning of "anomie," the idea of a society that leaves people without a clear sense of which norms to follow. A technical word is required to discuss a concept that has greater depth, precision, and generality than is normally present in a conversation.

4. These theories ask *second-order questions* that we do not usually bother with in everyday life. Second-order questions

have us stepping back from our direct interaction with the world (first order) and interrogating underlying assumptions about the nature of knowledge and the character of existence. They ask, for example, how we know certain things. A first-order question might simply ask if it is raining outside right now. But second-order thinking pushes past the surface to ask questions about how humans know the world around us. For example, we might ask if all human cultures think of rain the same way. The discussion of the social construction of reality above was an example of a second-order question about the character of human knowledge.

5. At the level of formal theory, we always *relate our own theoretical activity to existing bodies of knowledge*. In everyday theorizing, we can dream up whatever explanation we like for a particular event. In contrast, in formal theory, we either build on the foundation of existing theories or critique them to show their shortcomings. In this context, we do not begin from scratch, given that there have already been many attempts to explain whatever it is we are investigating.

These forms of rigour provide valuable tools for the evaluation of arguments and claims. Critical thinking is one of the capacities most prized in university graduates, as it is a crucial foundation for effective problem solving grounded in real knowledge rather than hope and speculation. One of the central aspects of critical thinking is to evaluate arguments, your own and those of others, using deliberately selected and widely recognized criteria. These five forms of rigour provide a particular set of criteria for evaluating formal theories; getting practice using these assessments of rigour will help develop critical thinking skills.

Developing some familiarity with these criteria will also help with your own research projects and essays. Students often think of university research projects as a treasure hunt through other people's writings. It seems as if you seek sources to find answers that you collect and arrange into a paper. Your professors, however, are often looking for your ability to make sense of the material. The forms of rigour described above will be useful in assessing your own success at making a case in papers you write.

It is not the claim of this book that formal theorizing is the ultimate form of knowledge that trumps all others. There are many ways of knowing that yield valuable results. However, an engagement with formal theory will help you become more deliberate in your own choices about knowledge, whether you adopt any of the positions discussed here or reject them all.

Thinking Point: Knowing Your Sources

Find both a newspaper article and an **academic source** that cover an issue related to poverty. Use the five criteria for rigour in formal theories to compare these sources. What conclusions can you draw about the character of newspaper writing in relation to formal scholarly research?

3

But How Do You Know?

THERE IS nothing more human than the need to find things out. This is confirmed by watching children at play, as they explore the world around them and seek explanations for the phenomena they experience. It can become quite irksome for parents and caregivers to deal with the always-present question, "Why?" But, as Jenny Diski argues, it is difficult to fault a child's inquisitive spirit, for inquiry is, after all, what children specialize in. In Diski's words, "children are born spies." It is their "sole task . . . to find out what is going on," a task that includes both straightforward demands for answers and a good deal of undercover work (Diski 2008, 11). Although most of us gradually lose the confidence to ask "why" every time we don't understand something, we never fully lose the drive to find things out. In our own ways, then, we are all experts in inquiry.

Some traditional academic approaches draw a clear distinction between how we inquire and learn in everyday life and how we do so in scholarly research. By contrast, the starting point for this chapter is that academic inquiry is not separate from the forms of inquiry in which you already engage on a daily basis. Certainly there are important differences between academic inquiry and inquiry in everyday life; however, these differences come down to variations in the quest for knowledge as opposed to marking borders between completely separate activities.

By emphasizing the continuity between everyday knowledge and academic inquiry, this chapter builds on one of the important contributions of feminist research. Marjorie DeVault, for example, argues that the central ideas of feminism arose "from systematic attention to previously unacknowledged experiences that women began to speak of together." Feminist inquiry takes seriously the everyday knowledge exchanged between women. "Its character as a public movement insists that women's talk is not mere gossip or folklore, but rather the basis for grounded knowledge of experiences obscured and distorted in the past; its aims include revealing and refining such knowledges" (DeVault 1999, 2–3). In light of the fact that feminist inquiry aims to contribute to the liberation of women, it makes sense that it would not want to dismiss the knowledge that women already have. Feminist researchers seek to build upon everyday knowledge with the purpose of revealing hidden or unacknowledged insights and refining those understandings through more methodical approaches.

Inquiry helps us find where we're going, how to get what we want, how to know what we need to know. We navigate the world—we make sense of it—through inquiry. New students on a university campus often find themselves engaged deeply in processes of inquiry simply to find a classroom or a particular office. What this chapter intends to show is that the same inquiry skills that helped you find the door of the class are also useful inside the room. The trick, however, to translating our familiar patterns of inquiry into the kind that best suits academic research is to make our processes of inquiry more methodical.

METHODICAL RESEARCH

THE INQUIRY we conduct on a daily basis—to find our way to a coffee spot for the first time, for example—is generally personal and unstructured. There are certainly patterns in these practices: for instance, the gendered tendency for women to ask for directions and for men to muddle through a long series of missteps. The decisions, however, are not generally conscious choices made by deliberately weighing alternate possibilities. In contrast to everyday inquiry, method, at its core, is about conscious choices and systematic approaches.

Being methodical—clarifying our choices and reflecting on our movements step by step—allows us to become more conscious of what we know and how we know it. It makes it easier to explain, reflect upon, and revise the processes through which knowledge is generated.

Method is the basis of rigour, which, at first, seems a rather forbidding term. The *OED Online* (2009) defines rigour at a general level as "severity in dealing with a person or persons; extreme strictness; harshness." The more specific meaning of rigour is "strict accuracy, severe exactitude." All that strictness and exactitude can sound pretty cold. But, despite appearances, being methodical is not simply about laying down a bunch of petty rules and following them to the letter; rather, it is about being more transparent and effective in generating knowledge.

In our everyday lives, people rarely ask the question, "But how do you know what you know?" The trusting relationships we build over time, as well as the cultural constraints on persistent questioning, mean that a great deal of what we hear and say on a daily basis is accepted (or rejected) without deep thought. By contrast, at the core of the specialized knowledge-generating processes associated with academic research is a commitment to always having an answer to the question, "How do you know?" In formal research, unlike in everyday conversation, it is essential to describe as clearly and thoroughly as possible not only our major conclusions—the sum of the cases we put forward—but each step of the research process and why those steps were chosen in the first place. This approach is very different from the typical line of argument used to explain to a friend why you liked the original *Transformers* better than the sequels. Methodical inquiry demands that you clarify the relationship between the process of gathering facts and the process of interpreting the facts that you've gathered. As such, the process is best thought of as a cycle of inquiry.

POWERS OF DEDUCTION

THE POWER of doing methodical inquiry was one of the key themes of the old Sherlock Holmes stories. Sherlock Holmes was an early fictional detective, famous for his big mind and rigorous inquiry. He was certainly no action hero but, rather, focused on meticulous investigation. He was accompanied by his sidekick Watson, who got to see the key elements of every investigation but could never figure out the case on his own.

In the story "A Scandal in Bohemia," Watson expressed admiration for Holmes's superior investigative power, noting that he could shadow Holmes through a whole case and still be awed by his ability to draw a conclusion:

> When I hear you give your reasons . . . the thing always appears to me to be so ridiculously simple that I could easily do it myself, though at each successive instance of your reasoning I am baffled, until you explain your process. And yet I believe that my eyes are as good as yours. (Conan Doyle 1976, 2)

Holmes begins to clue us into his method, telling Watson, "You see, but you do not observe" (Conan Doyle 1976, 2). There is more to inquiry than just seeing. Scrupulous observation is important, but there is another element to Holmes's method, which he calls **deduction**. He describes his method to Watson as, "I see it. I deduce it" (Conan Doyle 1976, 1). According to the *OED Online* (2009), to deduce is "to derive or draw as a conclusion from something already known or assumed; to derive by a process of reasoning or inference." There is something beyond the collection of facts that leads to a conclusion, some process of connecting the facts to an explanation through reasoning and/or inference.

Holmes's process of deduction is basically one of theorization. He argues that theory must come *after* the facts are accumulated, to avoid bias. "It is a capital mistake to theorize before one has data. Insensibly one begins to twist facts to suit theories, instead of theories to suit facts" (Conan Doyle 1976, 3). As we will see in this book, there are other approaches to this relationship of theory and fact.

Holmes's powers of deduction are so great that they can sometimes seem mystical. Watson at one point suggests that the detective seems to display almost supernatural powers that would have got him in big trouble in previous generations: "You would certainly have been burned, had you lived a few centuries ago" (Conan Doyle 1976, 2). In the end, however, there is no witchcraft, only methodical inquiry. Structured research forms an important part of numerous professions: journalism, detective work, legal practice, medical science, and environmental engineering, just to name a few.

Sherlock Holmes provides us with a good introduction to the two essential components of methodical inquiry. First, there must be a thorough process of fact gathering and documentation. Second, these facts must be drawn together and explained through the use of theory. In the end, Holmes's ability to make a case about who committed the crime combines investigation and analysis.

THE QUALITY OF EVIDENCE

P EOPLE TEND not to be particularly picky about the quality of evidence in their daily lives. There is rarely reason or time to pause and reflect on how you know a specific fact or what sources to trust. People do not hesitate to weigh in on the sex-partner choices of a celebrity or the guilt of someone accused of a high-profile crime. It is common to hear people talk about the role of human nature in all kinds of activities. In day-to-day conversations, the only real standard of proof is whether you can say it without being seriously challenged. Because it is so prevalent and often based on rich experiences, this unsystematic knowledge is highly useful and not to be casually dismissed.

However, the unsystematic nature of this knowledge means that it contains many great insights mixed in with errors and misinterpretations. Certainly, you would not want to be convicted of a crime simply because a lot of people thought you did it. There are many places in our society where methodical inquiry is required to make a case. Academic disciplines in the university are one example, but there are many others. All of them share, at some level, the Sherlock Holmes method of combining investigation and analysis, or "I see it. I deduce it."

The courtroom is one of the places where the rules of methodical inquiry are most clearly laid out. It does not go very far in a legal case to say, "I know he is guilty." The next question is sure to be, "How do you know?" Indeed, much of the process of a criminal trial is dedicated to sorting out the basic facts of a case.

We have all been in a situation with friends where we dispute each other's accounts of what actually happened. The aim of a court case is to sort through these contending stories to find the most solid factual basis possible for making a legal decision. A courtroom is filled with many legal experts, yet a crucial decision-making role in many criminal trials is accorded to a panel of non-experts, the jury. Not surprisingly, the job of the jury is not to make judgements about the fine points of law. Rather, it has to evaluate the facts. According to Paciocco and Stuesser (2008, 1), judges are "triers of law," and juries are "triers of fact."

In the courtroom, you cannot simply make any assertion and back it up through sheer bravado. There, facts must be backed by evidence: "Evidence of a fact is information that tends to prove it" (Paciocco and Stuesser 2008, 1). The rules governing evidence provide a framework for resolving questions of fact by providing criteria for assessing the basis for any knowledge claim. For example, evidence is categorized as either direct or circumstantial. Of these, direct is the most powerful as it "establishes a material fact without the need for any inferences to be drawn" (Paciocco and Stuesser 2008, 31). Direct evidence, for example, might be the testimony of someone who personally witnessed the act in question or a clear photograph of the act. Of course, such evidence could still be challenged, but, if it stands, it connects the person directly to the act.

In contrast, circumstantial evidence requires inferences, meaning that it suggests links but does not make indisputable connections. For example, if someone were to testify that she had seen the accused leaving a restaurant in the vicinity of the act in question, a link might be inferred but no direct connection would be established. Circumstantial evidence, if it is relevant, might help establish a case but cannot fully support it. That is why investigators spend so much time in cop shows mucking through garbage-filled dumpsters to find specific pieces of evidence, such as the murder weapon.

The rules of evidence exclude hearsay evidence, so one person cannot quote the words of another who is not present for cross-examination. The problem is "the inability to test the reliability of hearsay statements" (Paciocco and Stuesser 2008, 104). People can observe the bearing and tone of a witness giving live testimony in the courtroom; furthermore, that witness can be cross-examined to assess the basis of her statements. The principle of cross-examination is the importance of subjecting evidence to rigorous scrutiny. Cross-examination means that every claim to knowledge can be thoroughly evaluated.

The character of cross-examination is reflected even in the manner of questioning witnesses that is permitted. In general, leading questions (questions that either suggest a specific answer or a set of facts that have never been established) are excluded in favour of open-ended questions that leave a witness room to respond without constraints (Paciocco and Stuesser 2008, 412–13). Cross-examination is less restricted than initial testimony, as witnesses are called by one side in legal proceedings specifically to establish facts that make a case, and the goal of the other side is to subject such evidence to rigorous scrutiny. Thus, leading questions during cross-examination are "entirely permissible, and counsel are well advised to lead as a means of controlling the testimony of these adversary witnesses" (Paciocco and Stuesser 2008, 427).

All these courtroom rules and procedures are not there simply to mystify proceedings and keep lawyers employed, even if it might sometimes seem that way. They are there because they impose standards for making a case. In everyday conversation, facts and opinions are easily intertwined. In court, by contrast, opinions are generally inadmissible, as legal decisions must be made on the basis of facts and not speculation. The one admissible form of opinion in the courtroom is that of an acknowledged expert, as regular jury members "lack the experience of the expert on the matter in question and therefore require assistance in knowing what to make of the facts" (Paciocco and Stuesser 2008, 184). The expert, in short, is allowed to venture opinions as these might assist the jury members in making sense of the facts.

One of the key features of methodical research is that knowledge claims are subjected to scrutiny. The specific conventions of the courtroom are not the same as those of the essay or of journalism, but the underlying principle is consistent. First, one must always be conscious of *how* one knows what is known. Second, the quality of sources and documentation is assessed within a framework that defines a specific way of doing inquiry.

JUST THE FACTS?

ONE OF the central issues in methodical research is the stance of the investigator, the extent to which the person conducting the inquiry should claim to be neutral and disinterested. In a courtroom, lawyers do not pretend to be unbiased players in the cases before them; rather, they are very clearly biased in favour of their clients. By contrast, one of the central claims of the modern journalist is the commitment to uncovering and disseminating facts in a neutral fashion. According to a reporter for the Toronto *Globe and Mail*, the job of the journalist is to "report on what happened in neutral language, and let the reader sort out who was right and who was wrong" (MacKinnon 2005, 92). The media critic Barrie Gunter (1997, 9) agrees, writing that "at the heart of all good journalism lies the practice of objective reporting. This means giving a full and accurate account of events being reported which reflects as closely as possible the true facts of a matter."

The claim here is that journalistic investigation consists of impartial inquiry performed by trained minds in the public interest. Journalism depicts itself as uniquely capable of doing methodical inquiry in a way that produces an objective or unbiased view of current affairs. Most of us are so familiar with the civic importance of **objectivity** in news that it can be surprising to discover that this particular way of knowing the world is a relatively recent historical development. In fact, prior to the late 1800s, anything that would be recognized as printed news today could only be described as decidedly non-objective.

For example, Paul Nesbitt-Larking (2007, 36) tells us that in mid-1800s Canada, there was a "vibrant press" supporting the rule of the "Family Compact" and, by contrast, a different one supporting reformers who "railed against absentee landownership and feudal political arrangements." Neither of the two journalistic camps attempted even-handedness: the newspaper of the ruling class clearly and unapologetically advocated the ideas of the ruling class; that of the reformers and radicals clearly and unapologetically advocated the ideas of reform and revolution. This era of journalism in North America and Europe is often called the era of the "partisan press" because individual newspapers tended to serve as mouthpieces for specific political parties.

Between the 1890s and 1930s, objectivity replaced partisanship as the primary aim of journalism (Sotiron 1997). Contrary to what you might expect, however, the emerging commitment to fair and balanced reporting grew out of competition among newspapers for advertising dollars, not from some ancient devotion to truth and light. Newspaper owners realized that they could make more money by selling advertising space to private companies than by selling subscriptions to readers. Advertisers tend to care less about the political beliefs of newspaper readers than about placing ads in publications with high circulation. Mindful of the need to attract advertisers, newspapers began focusing on ways of attracting ever-larger audiences. One of the best ways of doing so was to produce news coverage that would be deemed trustworthy by a vast and varied group of readers. Moving away from their traditional political positions, then, newspapers developed ways of methodical reporting that helped depict journalists as disinterested and balanced observers.

Critics have argued that it is impossible to achieve objective journalism within the profit-driven framework that governs the production of mainstream news today. Ericson, Baranek, and Chan (1989), for instance, have written that as long as objective journalism is undertaken within a system devoted to offending as few people as possible and as long as fairness and accuracy are equated with the uncritical reporting of two sides of every issue, then objective journalism will serve to protect the dominant interests in society. This version of methodical inquiry, which relies heavily upon neutral language, expert testimony from official sources, and quotations from competing parties in dispute, will consistently exclude or delegitimize those ideas and voices that lie outside the mainstream culture.

Gillmor (2006) argues that, in the age of the Internet, people are increasingly rejecting the kind of news produced by "objective" news organizations and, instead, are seeking out news produced by so-called citizen journalists. Developments in information and communication technologies have opened up new possibilities for people to communicate directly with each other, and citizens are more and more frequently serving as journalists in ways previously unknown—and ways not always available to professional reporters. "The Internet provides a ready vehicle for groups that wish to democratize the media" (Smith 2010, 214), and, all around the world, citizens are taking advantage. Personal narratives appearing on blogs, videos posted on YouTube, and other do-it-yourself modes of journalism have an aura of authenticity that big media producers lack. The reigning journalistic process of inquiry (objective journalism) is being challenged by a grass-roots movement committed to a different way of generating knowledge.

It is exciting to think about the potential of citizen journalism to make up for some of the shortcomings of objective journalism; yet it is important to ask whether there may be losses associated with the decline of traditional journalism's commitment to objectivity. Eric Alterman argues that the decline of the daily newspaper is dangerous for democracy. He points out that a newspaper's unique combination of resources, expert reporters, and the drive to discover the truth has been essential in uncovering abuses of political power over the past century. As Alterman (2008, 59) writes, "Just how an Internet-based news culture can spread the kind of 'light' that is necessary to prevent terrible things, without the armies of reporters and photographers that newspapers have traditionally employed, is a question that even the most ardent democrat . . . may not wish to see answered." He concludes that, although it is important to criticize the news industry's role in perpetuating systematic forms of discrimination, we ought to think twice before abandoning the processes and communication networks used to pursue objective news.

INQUIRY AND THE BASIS OF KNOWLEDGE

Both inquiry in the courts and journalistic inquiry are methodical ways of pursuing objectivity. Yet, despite the fact that the two professions have developed processes for uncovering truth, these processes are not identical. Consider the role of experts in the two contexts. It's true that the courts allow the testimony of expert witnesses, but even experts testify on behalf of either the prosecution or the defence; and experts are subject to cross-examination. By contrast, the opinions of experts are frequently used by journalists to establish the indisputable facts of a matter. In the newspaper, quotations from experts can be used to enhance a story's appearance of disinterest and balance.

As the movement for citizen journalism demonstrates, even within the two professions there are fundamental debates about the best way to gather facts and the conditions necessary to uncover truth. It is debates of this sort that frame assumptions about how we do methodical inquiry. And although with a bit of effort we can see these debates simmering beneath the surface in the workings of journalism, the courts, and a range of political institutions, it is in the realm of academic research that they are articulated most clearly.

The reason academics are so concerned about what people take for granted when they do inquiry is that these assumptions determine in large part what exactly it is that we study, as well as shape the methods used to generate knowledge. It follows, then, that, in academic research, it is crucial to be conscious of the implications of the choices you make in a process of inquiry. These choices are often made on the basis of explicit or implicit conceptions of knowledge.

Theories of knowledge clarify a researcher's assumptions about what it is possible to know in the world. In the social sciences, there are three major schools of thought about knowledge and inquiry: the positivist, interpretive, and critical approaches. These models have very different views of the relation between our own subjective activity and the world of objects outside our heads that we investigate.

Positivist

Positivist social science argues that inquiry involves the empirical examination of a world of objects that exists independent of our activity. As a theory of knowledge, positivism holds that "the only genuine or legitimate knowledge claims are those founded directly on experience" (Schwandt 2007, 233). The premise of positivism, therefore, is that it is possible to use our senses to explore neutrally the objects around us, in part by rigorously controlling for **subjectivity** and bias.

The Cycle of Inquiry

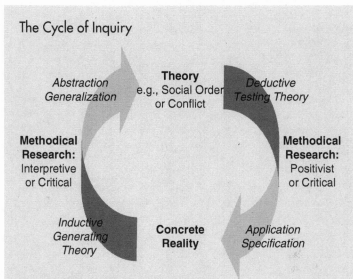

Abstraction
Generalization

Theory
e.g., Social Order
or Conflict

Deductive
Testing Theory

**Methodical
Research:**
Interpretive
or Critical

**Methodical
Research:**
Positivist
or Critical

Inductive
Generating
Theory

**Concrete
Reality**

Application
Specification

Figure 3.1 The Cycle of Inquiry

This illustration traces out the cycle of inquiry, pictured as an ongoing movement between concrete reality and theoretical thinking. The cycle moves through both inductive and deductive phases, producing maps that can guide us through the complexities of reality.

The **inductive** phase begins with the observation of reality and moves towards theory through processes of abstraction (identifying and highlighting the crucial elements for analysis) and generalization (seeking out patterns that apply to a number of cases). The inductive phase of research is concerned primarily with generating theory to explain specific phenomena identified through the observation of concrete reality.

The **deductive** phase begins with theoretical explanations and moves towards concrete reality through processes of application (putting the theory to use in a specific context) and specification (identifying what theoretical concepts will look like in a particular setting or operationalizing terms through precise, observable definitions, for example, spelling out the precise parameters for "poverty"). The deductive phase is concerned primarily with testing theories, assessing their adequacy in explaining actual events.

Positivist approaches to research tend to emphasize primarily the deductive phase of the cycle of inquiry, seeking to test theories through application and evaluation. In contrast, interpretive approaches generally focus on inductive research, working out theoretical explanations to actual events that researchers have experienced. Critical approaches tend to draw on both inductive and deductive research processes. In reality, most research processes combine elements of inductive and deductive reasoning.

The adoption of core theoretical premises, such as social order or conflict theory, frames both deductive and inductive research processes as they sensitize observers to certain phenomena and direct attention away from others. There is rich debate within the social sciences about the possibility of conducting objective or disinterested research.

Methodical inquiry is founded on the meticulous collection of high-quality sense data. Among other things, this means that you must document clearly the system you are using to gather data. If you are observing people eating chocolate to see if it makes them happy, you must make absolutely clear the criteria you are using to assess their mood as they consume the product.

Positivism can seem pretty obvious at first glance. If you're asked to describe the space you are in right now, you are most likely to begin cataloguing the sight, smell, sound, taste, or feel of things that surround you. It seems that your senses allow you to record bits of the reality around you and then convert that data into words to piece together a report. This process matches the positivist goal of research, which is to "capture" a chunk of external reality, in much the same way as a photograph grabs an image of a scene (Eliot 2006).

Indeed, photography has served as a model for positivist research. In the late 1800s, some scientists saw photography as the basis for a whole new kind of objectivity in research. The scientist could step out of the equation and use a machine to record the evidence. The camera's apparent removal of the human observer fit with the idea that objectivity required restraint, holding back subjective judgements to allow the simple truth to be captured:

> . . . all-too-human scientist[s] must, as a matter of duty, restrain themselves from imposing their hopes, expectations, generalizations, aesthetics, even ordinary language on the image of nature. Where human self-discipline flagged, the machine would take over. (Daston and Galison 1992, 81)

The aim of the positivist approach is ultimately to develop laws that allow science to predict phenomena by identifying regularities in the observable patterns of the world around us (Keat and Urry 1982, 4–5). The rigorous collection of objective sense data allows us to detect patterns of connection that can then be explained theoretically, connections, for example, between the freezing of water and its increase in volume or between the dominant social class of a particular voting region and how that region will vote in an election.

Interpretive

Interpretive social science challenges the obviousness of positivism. If you're asked to describe the space you are in, the process you go through in achieving the description might not be quite as simple as it seems. You do not simply record bits of sound, sight, or smell, but you assign categories and make interpretations. In contrast to positivist research, the interpretive approach does not seek to uncover universal truths about social reality that exist outside our heads but to better understand how reality is constructed through language, culture, institutions, and interactions among people. The interpretive approach assumes the social world is largely "what people perceive it to be" (Neuman 2000, 72) and aims to draw generalizations about human life by studying those perceptions.

The interpretive approach leads to a different understanding of photographs than positivism—seeing them as constructed images rather than objective documents. Photographs seem to have amazing documentary power, as they appear to eliminate mediation and make us first-hand observers of events distant in time and space. Indeed, they are considered so potent that their use as evidence is specifically regulated in court. As Paciocco and Stuesser (2008, 460) write, "photographs or videotapes are powerful pieces of evidence, and they may be excluded where they would serve to inflame the minds of jurors against the accused." There is something about an image that has particular inflammatory power.

This inflammatory power is, in part, based on the sensation photographs offer of first-hand observation. If we tell you about the injuries a person sustained in a fight, you have only a second-hand relationship with them through our narrative. You are always conscious of our mediation, our role as storyteller. If, in contrast, we show you a picture of a bloodied and broken face, you might feel a kind of direct and unmediated relationship. You can explore with your own eyes and are not limited by the details we choose to relay or withhold.

And yet the photograph does not really give you first-hand access. Every photograph involves processes of selection, freezing a particular moment in time and space. Any picture tells you only the tiniest bit of the story. Indeed, it may not even tell the true story at all. Wedding photos, for example, show smiling faces of carefully groomed people posed in picturesque settings. The real stories are often carefully hidden in these pictures, even if we leave aside specific issues of image manipulation.

Photographic images, then, confront us with a dilemma: they grant us the feeling of first-hand access but, in fact, offer up a constructed document, made up both during the immediate moment of taking the picture and then again through processes of finishing. The interpretive approach to research generalizes this understanding. Just as photographs might seem to be objective documents, so research might claim only to document the world around us. Interpretive approaches remind us of the important and inescapable role of subjectivity as we frame, select, and interpret the world.

Critical

Finally, **critical social science** combines elements of both the positivist and interpretive approach. It shares with positivism the conviction that people do have access to the world outside their own subjective activity, which can be explored through the senses. It shares with the interpretive approach the idea that access to the world is always mediated by subjective activity—our culture, language, and place in society—so that every investigation depends on the viewpoint of the researcher.

The critical perspective understands photographs both as documents of reality and as subjective constructions. The Canadian photographer Jeff Wall aligns with the critical perspective when he argues that it is important to challenge the two dominant myths about photographs: the first, that photos tell the truth and the second, that they do not, as they are fabrications (Edwards 2006, 117). The critical perspective argues that a photograph can combine truth *and* fabrication. Steve Edwards (2006, 117) urges us to preserve the tension between the photograph as truth and as artifice, recognizing that both elements in fact coexist in the practice of photography. Photographs, for example, have an important part to play in documenting injustices:

> While there are very good reasons to be suspicious of the supposed neutrality and objectivity of photographs, there is a danger of throwing out the proverbial baby with the bathwater . . . photographs are likely to continue to play a prominent role in contesting the effects of power. (Edwards 2006, 116)

Critical social science invites us to challenge both the myth of the impartial researcher, as associated with positivism, and the conception of research as completely subjective, as associated with interpretive approaches. "Critical social science says that to deny that a researcher has a point of view [as positivists do] is itself a point of view" (Neuman 2000, 81). At the core of the critical approach is the idea that every inquiry yields a partial answer, in the dual sense that it is only part of the picture and is based on only a particular perspective. Yet this partial picture does capture a reality, even if only a part of it from a particular viewpoint. It is possible to investigate the objective world that exists independent of us, but it is not possible to do that without subjectivity.

The goal of critical social science is to probe beneath the surface of things, to get at the "structures and mechanisms which causally generate the observable phenomena . . . which allows us to explain them" (Keat and Urry 1982, 5). Positivist approaches seek to predict events, interpretive approaches to understand the meanings they hold, and critical approaches to explain them.

Postmodern Critiques of Science

Positivist, interpretive, and critical approaches each claim to offer a better way to find out and a set of methods that provides a more solid basis for knowledge claims. Postmodern approaches raise a more fundamental question, asking whether it is even possible to know. Scholarly disciplines tend to understand knowledge as a hierarchy, classifying different ways of knowing as more or less solid and reliable. Each of these disciplines has developed a set of practices or methods yielding knowledge that is regarded as sound. There may, of course, be disputes within disciplines about which method is better, as exemplified in the discussion of positivist, interpretive, and critical approaches. But there is general agreement that sound knowledge is possible, even if there is no consensus about how to get there.

In contrast, postmodernists challenge the whole idea of the hierarchy of knowledge that classifies certain methods as more reliable. Lyotard (1984, 39) argues that, since the late 1800s, sciences have experienced an "internal erosion of the legitimacy principle of knowledge." The claim that scientific knowledge was better than other ways of knowing was undermined over time.

In part, this erosion of legitimacy occurred because scientific knowledge claimed to be neutral but, in fact, reflected the position of the powerful. Lyotard (1984, 8–9) writes that "knowledge and power are simply two sides of the same question." This relationship between knowledge and power is made obvious in the colonial context, where science is understood as the tool of the colonizer. Gayatri Spivak (1999, 216), in her analysis of colonial documents, notes that science is used in a very particular way: "The science in question here is the 'interested' science of war rather than 'disinterested' knowledge as such." The job of this science is to distinguish the master from the native: "The manipulation of the pedagogy of this science is also in the 'interest' of creating what will come to be perceived as a 'natural' difference between the 'master' and the 'native'—a difference in human or racial material." Ultimately this is a science in which the master is cast as the knower and the native as the known: "The master is the subject of science or knowledge."

Rather than producing unique claims to knowledge grounded in science or any other discipline, postmodernism focuses on the critical encounter with all forms of knowledge, asking about (or "interrogating") how all presuppositions and ways of framing the world yield specific insights and block others. Lyotard (1984, 60) argues that postmodern science concerns itself with "such things as undecidables, the limits of precise control, conflicts characterized by incomplete information" and therefore produces "not the known, but the unknown." According to postmodernism, all forms of human knowledge are simply stories we tell ourselves, none of which have any more intrinsic merit than any others. The focus of postmodernism is therefore more on the critique of all knowledge claims than on the generation of new ones.

DISCIPLINING YOUR OWN RESEARCH

At this point, you may be wondering why all this matters. This kind of detailed focus on something that seems fairly obvious might seem academic, in the worst sense of irrelevant hair-splitting. But the goal here is to give you tools to use in your own processes of inquiry. One of the key things you can learn in your postsecondary education is to become a more effective problem solver by getting better at figuring things out.

As a starting point, that means thinking about the work you are doing *as* inquiry. Reading the research done by others, for example, is not simply a matter of absorption, as a sponge does to water; it means taking apart, assessing, and reintegrating information with what you already know. You will find it easier to understand the contributions of sources you read if you reflect on their own framing assumptions, especially by asking whether they are using a positivist, interpretive, or critical approach.

The goal is for you to become more methodical in your own inquiry. Thinking about theories of knowledge can also help you become more aware of the choices you are making in your research. Although high-level conceptions such as "positivism" are unlikely to find their way into your everyday conversations, thinking about what these terms mean should make it easier to reflect upon strategies you use in even the most basic research process. To put it bluntly, thinking about theories of knowledge will help to discipline your own inquiry.

The decision to use the word "discipline" here is a conscious one, and not only because a great deal of schooling is about discipline. Rather, the word carries different meanings, which, you will soon see, is why it is useful in this conversation. By examining the alternative meanings of the word discipline, we begin to see some key tensions surrounding methodical inquiry in the university.

According to the *OED Online* (2009), discipline originally meant "to instruct, educate, train." From this perspective, disciplined inquiry evokes an image of thoughtful, systematic, well-reasoned documentation and explanation. However, the *OED* also notes that, over time, the word has become associated not only with training in a general sense but also with training "to habits of order and subordination." From this contrasting perspective, disciplined inquiry evokes an image of uncritical rule following, strict limitations on curiosity, and elitist definitions of legitimate research. Like the word discipline itself, disciplined inquiry in practice is home to tensions between productive rigour on one hand and stifling conventions on the other.

The idea of disciplined inquiry is built right into the structure of postsecondary education. Universities are structured around academic "disciplines" (psychology and geography, for example), each of which has its own conventions for rigorous research. One of the challenges for university students is to figure out what each academic discipline involves. Life outside the university does not prepare you to distinguish, for example, between archaeology and anthropology or between political science and sociology. Does the French Department teach language skills and the English Department literature?

The most common assumption to make when confronted with a wide variety of academic disciplines vying for your interest is to assume that they are defined primarily by their specific area of study: astronomy looks at stars, political science at governments, and philosophy at trees falling in forests when no one is there. Actually, an academic discipline is defined by both the specific field of study it examines and the specific methods it uses to explore this field. The same field might be explored by different disciplines, often in quite different ways. For example, the past is not the sole province of history departments at universities but is also examined by English departments (which tend to focus on literature), linguistics departments (which look at the evolution of language over time), and archaeology departments (which try to uncover the past by understanding the objects left behind by human societies).

Unfortunately, academic disciplines are often presented as repositories of existing knowledge rather than as ways of finding things out. In this model, the job of the student is simply to digest the existing knowledge and spit it out again on request. Here we see the negative definition of discipline raising its ugly head. However, academic disciplines are more usefully understood as frameworks for inquiry, so that the job of the student is to find things out by using the discipline's unique analytical perspective and tools. It is true that disciplines can seem overly restrictive and conservative, but they remain important ways of bringing conceptual focus and coherence to the generation of knowledge. Although the negative aspects of disciplined inquiry are often the easiest to see, the positive ones remain present. The enabling quality of disciplined research is clarified as we focus upon the conceptual structures and technical procedures provided by formal **research methods.**

THE ROLE OF METHOD

IF YOU look up "declutter" online, you will be immersed in tips on how to tidy your room. This raises a basic question: Do we really need tips on how to clean up? Is it not just a question of effort? Of course, effort is required, and we all know people who are more or less motivated to tidy. But these "decluttering" websites suggest there may be more involved. Indeed, there is a category of "declutter professionals," whose job is to teach you key principles in organizing your spaces. The impact of effort is always magnified through method, through organized ways of approaching a problem.

The *OED Online* (2009) defines method generally as "a procedure for attaining an object." In the case of a messy office, "method" refers to the section-by-section approach that we might use to bring order to the room. Other people might use a different method; for example, they might take care of garbage first, then clothes, then papers. We know a professor who uses a time-based cleaning method: she straightens anything that she can get her hands on in 15-minute spurts; she takes a 2-minute break and then goes back in for more cleaning. There are a variety of methods that can be used to attain a clean room. And there are a variety of methods that researchers use to attain knowledge about the world.

Whether you realize it or not, you've probably heard the names of at least a handful of research methods, and you may even have had some experience using formal methods. For example, if you've ever conducted an interview as a way of learning more about a topic or a specific person's experiences, then you've used a method. Even if you were in Grade Two at the time, and you were interviewing your great-uncle about his enormous collection of teddy bears, you were using a well-established, suitable research method. A method is defined by the process of examination it follows, not by the topic being examined and not by the credentials of the person using the method. A commercial for face wash claiming that its surveys show that 84 per cent of teenagers prefer Brand X to Brand Y relies upon the method of surveying. City workers who count the number of people sitting in a park over the lunch hour are using the method of observation.

The reason we use methods is to add rigour to our work of generating knowledge about the world around us. A research method, then, is not simply a process of examination but a process of examination meant to aid in the collection and interpretation of trustworthy knowledge. Neuman (2000, 5) writes that social research "is more than a collection of methods and a process for creating new knowledge; it is a process for producing new knowledge about the social world that uses a scientific approach." If we wanted to write a book about the state of law enforcement in North America, we could watch the movie *Mall Cop*, read the Wikipedia entry on "police," recall the time James was ticketed for jaywalking, and get down to writing. But chances are that people would ask a few questions about whether we were using the right methods to reach our conclusions in light of the overall aim of the book.

Evaluating information is one of the most important elements of being methodical in inquiry. The parallel to the courtroom is instructive here. The effective use of witnesses in a court case requires that one anticipate the possible lines of cross-examination the other side might use. Similarly, a methodical researcher must anticipate the questions of someone who doubts or challenges the research. It is often more persuasive to engage in dialogue with other perspectives on the matter than to dismiss these casually or ignore them altogether. It is important to know how authoritative a source is, something that varies according to the conventions that govern the research project you are doing. The conventions for market research are different from those of academic research, and those of photojournalism are different from those of art photography for galleries.

Methods serve two main purposes: first, they provide templates of techniques for generating knowledge; and second, they furnish researchers with a way of responding to questions about how they arrived at the knowledge in their studies. By using established, rigorous methods of inquiry, researchers are better able to answer the question, "But how do you know?" But how do we know which methods to use? Why does social science inquiry sometimes use interviews and sometimes use surveys? In what ways can we assess the strength of a particular book's methods? Which methods are the right ones for you?

Although it is true that there are a variety of methods to choose from, choosing methods is not the same as choosing pizza toppings: the decision is driven by more than matters of individual taste. In fact, the question of which methods are most appropriate for a particular study cannot be separated from the theories of knowledge discussed in the last section. Professors sometimes talk about how their research methods will "emerge" from their theoretical approach, that is, whether they subscribe to a positivist, interpretive, or critical theory of knowledge. The suggestion is that our theories of knowledge inform our research questions, which, in turn, inform our research methods. Although the image of spontaneous growth conjured by the word "emerge" has the regrettable effect of concealing a process that tends to take hours of thinking, planning, revising, and replanning, it is true that different methods fit better with certain theories of knowledge than with others.

One of the core questions you need to ask yourself as you set out in a methodical process of inquiry is what type of information you want to gather. Social science research in general is oriented around two kinds of information. The first—*quantitative*—attempts to know the world through numbers.

Quantitative approaches assume that "the phenomenon we want to study is quantifiable" and proceed to sort data into specific categories in such a way as to turn them into numbers (Balnaves and Caputi 2001, 61). Quantitative approaches allow precise measurement and provide a strong basis for generalization. For example, the quantitative researcher inquires about voting intentions by conducting a large poll and concluding that 35 per cent of respondents say that they will vote for the Red Party. The precision of quantitative methods makes them appealing to positivists. "In quantitative research, observation is carried out from a position that is external to the subject studied, just as the 'scientific' observer adopts a neutral, detached stance" (Corbetta 2003, 39–40).

The second type of method, often called *qualitative*, provides rich accounts of human experience. The qualitative researcher "tries to get as deep inside the subject as possible, in an attempt to see social reality 'through the eyes of the subject studied'" (Corbetta 2003, 40). Rather than relying on numbers to tell the stories of people's lives—using sums of numerical data to make generalizations—qualitative studies are more likely to include longer quotations from interviews. As the qualitative sociologists Jody Miller and Barry Glasner (2004, 138) argue,

> All we sociologists have are stories. Some come from other people, some from our interactions with others. What matters is to understand how and where the stories are produced, which sort of stories they are, and how we can put them to honest and intelligent use in theorizing about social life.

Whereas quantitative data might allow us to predict how Canadians will vote on election day, qualitative approaches might give us a stronger sense of the process through which people decide how to vote. But regardless of whether research is based on qualitative or quantitative methods, one of the key elements of social scientific inquiry is a commitment to doing it ethically.

Thinking Point: Malinowski's Tent

Figure 3.2 Malinowski's Tent

Bronislaw Malinowski was an anthropologist early in the twentieth century who played an important role in the development of ethnography, or participant observation, as a qualitative research method. The idea of participant observation is that the researchers must share the experiences of people they are studying in order to understand them. If you want to understand what it is like to work at a fast-food workplace, you should do it for a while.

Here are three activities to help you think about participant observation and method in research.

1. Look carefully at the picture of Malinowski's tent (on the right), and reflect on what this tells you about his relationship with the people he was studying. Think about how much he was participating and how much he was observing.
2. Try doing a participant observational activity by going as a group to eat where other students are having a meal somewhere on your campus. After 20 minutes, each of you should write down notes on what you observed. Compare notes with each other, and assess the differences in your findings. Discuss a more methodical approach to this observation, one you might use next time.
3. Find a newspaper article and a scholarly article that cover the same issue. Compare the articles, describing, as best you can, the method used in each.

THE ETHICS OF METHODICAL INQUIRY

PEOPLE ARE not allowed to conduct research in the name of social science without considering the ethical dimensions of their project. The *OED Online* (2009) defines ethics as "the science of morals; the department of study concerned with the principles of human duty." More specifically, ethics is defined as "the rules of conduct recognized in certain associations or departments of human life." Ethics, then, explores the standards of conduct that accord with moral principles. Examples of ethical conduct might include telling the truth or shovelling your neighbour's snowy sidewalk; by contrast, unethical conduct might include lying or stealing your neighbour's patio furniture.

At first, the connection between research and ethics might not seem obvious. We are told from an early age that we shouldn't plagiarize the work of others and that we shouldn't lie about our own work. So, as long as we're ethical in those ways, isn't it a little extreme to worry about something as grand as moral principles when a research project does something as straightforward as, say, interview students about their university experiences? Maybe medical scientists ought to think about ethics before deciding to test new vaccines on children, but do social scientists need to worry about ethics?

It's true that medical and social science are significantly different; however, we mustn't forget that not all questions about university experience carry the same amount of potential risk. A question about personal experiences of violence is likely to generate greater risk than one about the quality of food in the cafeteria, as raising troubling questions can create real pain and suffering. When we consider the types of intrusions made by social researchers into people's lives, concerns about ethics in research on humans are unlikely to seem extreme.

Both individual universities and national research organizations have developed official codes of conduct for doing ethical research. For example, the fundamental statement of ethics for all university-based research in Canada was created by the three major Canadian research councils and is called

"The Tri-Council Policy Statement: Ethical Conduct for Research Involving Humans" (see http://www.pre.ethics.gc.ca/eng/policy-politique/initiatives/tcps2-eptc2/Default/ for the second edition of this policy statement). Northey, Tepperman, and Albanese (2009, 109) summarize some of the document's most important prescriptions, explaining, for example, what should and should not be done during social research:

> You must not exploit individuals or groups for personal gain and must recognize the debt you incur to the communities in which you work. You should be sensitive to the possible exploitation of individuals and groups in the research, and you should try to minimize the chance of such exploitation in the conduct of research. You must also be sensitive to cultural, individual, and role differences in studying groups of people with distinctive characteristics.

Neuman (2009, 66) adds that researchers must "never release harmful information about specific individuals collected for research purposes" and goes on to offer a simple but useful guiding principle: "Always show respect for the research participant."

The main point here echoes the central theme of this whole chapter, namely, that methodical research is best understood as a particular process of inquiry. And, in the case of interviews about university experiences, as in all social research, it is the process that needs to be ethical. It is possible to debate the appropriate level of oversight exercised by ethics review boards or to ask why social science undergraduates require written consent from their interview participants while journalism students needn't bother with consent forms when wandering the streets and asking questions. But it is beyond question that "you must balance potential benefits from research . . . against its potential costs" (Neuman 2009, 62). If a piece of research will not contribute very much to humanity, it does not justify intrusion into the lives of others. The more intrusive our research will be, the more it needs to be able to claim to deliver genuine benefits.

Social researchers must maintain a delicate balance between efficiency on the one hand and ethical conduct on the other. If you were conducting research on social behaviour in public washrooms, one very efficient and effective way to collect data would be to set up hidden cameras and watch the tapes. But because this approach would be highly intrusive, it could hardly be considered ethical. Ethical research requires that participants involved in a study have not only consented to participating but have given their *informed consent* to do so. In other words, participants must understand fully the aims and the potential risks of what they are being asked to do, as well as know that they have the right to quit the study at any point. The challenge of ensuring that informed consent has been properly achieved becomes all the more important when research participants are members of vulnerable groups such as children, prisoners, or people with mental illness.

In sum, research ethics are guidelines for monitoring not only the issues being researched but the ways in which research is conducted. The upshot of the emphasis on the process is that it becomes possible for you to do ethical research on controversial issues such as recreational drug use or assisted suicide; and, conversely, you can also do unethical research on much more benign topics such as book clubs, birdwatching, or bowling leagues. Again, it all comes down to whether your processes of inquiry are conducted in an ethical manner.

CONCLUSION

Oₙₑ OF the measures of learning is that you become more assured in your own processes of inquiry and thus deliberate in the choices you make. More than imitating or following instructions, you start to take charge of your own investigation. You evaluate for yourself the information or evidence you are collecting, applying relevant standards to assess its truth claims. You make conscious choices in framing assumptions, aware of the insights and limitations associated with the premises you adopt.

Indeed, one way to gauge an expert is the extent to which she or he is able to pursue a process of inquiry autonomously. Of course experts don't go it alone without ever consulting; indeed, awareness of one's own limitations is part of the toolkit of the expert. Knowledge generally develops through discussion and debate, not through isolation and invention. Nevertheless, the goal in becoming more adept at theoretical thinking and methodical research is to begin to take charge of your own processes of inquiry, whether formal (for example, for a course assignment) or informal (for example, to make a case against a garbage dump over a source of fresh water).

Notwithstanding Sherlock Holmes's compelling insights into the power of deduction ("I see it. I deduce it."), in fact, it is most useful not to think of inquiry as a one-way process that moves exclusively from theory to evidence, or the other way around, but rather as a cycle of inquiry moving constantly between richer empirical knowledge and more powerful generalizations. Holmes's deduction is one approach; **induction**, generalizing from what you see around you, is another.

In other words, you can enter the cycle of inquiry either at the top, in the area of sweeping generalizations, or at the bottom, immersed in the specific details of a particular situation. The goal is to keep moving through the cycle as your research progresses, clarifying your theoretical thinking as you seek to explain real events and deepening your understanding of the world around you as you apply powerful explanatory concepts. It is our nature as humans to begin any process with certain framing assumptions, and it is hoped that these are engaged in our investigation so we can confirm, reject, or modify them.

The central goal of this chapter is to provide some guidelines for engaging in effective inquiry, drawing on a variety of models. Sherlock Holmes served as a reminder that good research combines painstaking fact-finding and theoretical explanation. Legal rules of evidence provide a useful model of evaluating information, always raising the question, "How do you know?" Although cross-examination as such might not be a part of your research process, it is worth thinking about how someone wanting to challenge your case might raise questions about the nature of evidence that you will use to support your claims, whether "hearsay" evidence is really authoritative in everyday settings, and whether opinions are really persuasive without a firm grounding in methodically produced evidence.

Journalism provides an interesting case for thinking about the value and limitations of self-proclaimed objectivity in processes of inquiry. Those of us who seek to be informed about world events rely on journalism to provide coverage of happenings and circumstances beyond our experience. Good journalism can provide great insight through probing investigation and serious analysis. At the same time, however, the possibility and desirability of genuine disinterest is hotly contested.

It is precisely this kind of debate—asking whether or not it is possible to be unbiased—that frames the fundamental distinctions between the positivist, interpretive, and critical approaches to research. These systematic approaches to understanding how we know provide useful insights for reflecting on your own processes of inquiry and for critically reading the research of others. It is also important to be aware of the ethical character of your own research processes, whether that involves listening in on a conversation you are not meant to hear or asking people to share their painful memories.

Social order and conflict theories, discussed throughout the rest of this book, are not covered in this chapter. It is certainly interesting to think about the ways they might align with positivist, interpretive, and critical approaches; however, in the abstract, such thoughts would be an inevitably inconclusive exercise. There are, for example, conflict theorists who use positivist approaches to research, social order theorists who are primarily interpretive, and *vice versa*. At this point, the important thing is that you have begun to develop strategies to identify and discuss the fit between theory and research methods in a specific case, whether that case is an article you are reading or a project you are developing. The following chapter builds on these ideas about inquiry within the context of a familiar setting, namely, the typical university classroom.

4

You Are Here: Mapping Social Relations

IN MALLS, universities, and other confusing places there are often maps posted around to help you find your way. These maps sometimes include a very helpful spot marked "you are here." Of course, you knew where you could find yourself before you even looked at the map. The "you are here" dot is to help you locate yourself in an abstract representation of the space you are navigating. A map is a very good example of an **abstraction**, in which the unnecessary details are filtered out so that the key elements of the system (roads, rivers, walkways) stand out.

Social theories map the spaces we navigate, though in a rather different fashion than do mall directories. We must negotiate social relations just as we find our way around a mall, a school, a workplace, or a street. We must know when it is appropriate to make eye contact, pay money, clap our hands, follow orders, or sit in silence. Most of the time, we do all of this automatically without having to think about it. Only in a new situation, whether visiting another culture or entering a new setting, do we become conscious of the need to negotiate the expectations of others.

The aim of social theory is to make the complex web of social relations we negotiate every day visible to us. Investigating this web is necessary for two reasons. First, the familiarity of these relations means that we do not think about them. After you've had many years of schooling, for example, it simply makes sense to raise your hand before you speak, even though doing so at the dinner table might seem absurd. Second, just as the deep foundation that allows a tall building to keep standing is not obvious from the outside, so many key aspects of society are anchored in relations that are not immediately visible from the surface. Why would we want to cast a light upon these hidden social relations? For much the same reason that most people would choose a lighted alley over a dark one when walking around the city at night. Social theory helps us to chart our journey, to see where we are now and where we've come from, and to plot a path for where to go from here.

Social theories, then, offer some sort of map of social relations, but they seldom include a "you are here" spot. Indeed, it is often very hard to locate yourself at all in many social theories. They are taught in forbidding books as already completed systems that exist outside you, and they often operate at very high levels of abstraction, stripping away all the details and particularities that make a scene familiar and leaving only the key principles that are often unrecognizable from the perspective of participants.

This chapter is the "you are here" spot in this book. We are going to start in the classroom, which is likely the context in which you are reading this book. The classroom seems very obvious to those of us who have spent considerable portions of our lives in one. It seems to be a logical place in which to organize ourselves to learn. In this chapter, we will show how theoretical reflection allows things to be seen in the classroom that are not immediately obvious, and lets us ask how the organization of the educational system reflects the social relations of the broader society. We will start from the classroom as a physical space and work back to a broader view of the social relations of education.

The examination of the classroom through most of this chapter is from a critical perspective influenced by the conflict model. The aim is to challenge your assumptions and raise questions about a setting you might already take for granted. The "you are here" point in theory is the place where you are most likely to assume you know what you are seeing because it is all so familiar.

The chapter ends with an argument about education derived from the social order model. This application of theory will give you some experience in tracing key components of the argument back to the central premises of that theory. This exercise will help you understand the way formal theory frames your view of an issue, directing your view like binoculars so you can see certain things more clearly while cutting other things out.

INVESTIGATING THE CLASSROOM

Although we are both professors, we find it hard to sit still in most classrooms. The seats are usually hard and uncomfortable. The little writing tablet is often painfully awkward for Alan and others who are left-handed (unless you want to play the "Where's Waldo" game of hunting down one of the few left-handed places squirreled away somewhere in the room). James is no better at resisting email during a lecture than are many of his students. Frankly, we have to admit that we find it pretty hard to sit still and concentrate for the full length of most of the classes we teach.

If we have trouble sitting still in a classroom, it should not surprise us that some students shift, squirm, talk, sleep, or even get up from time to time. We do our best to silence restless students. A good classroom interaction requires that attention be concentrated on the teacher or whomever else is speaking. Indeed, one of our big frustrations is that students are particularly rude to other students who are speaking in the classroom, paying far less attention to them than they do to us.

So we do our job, which is to keep things under control. But we recognize the contradiction here: we daily expect our students to do something we cannot, which is sit still and let someone natter on for a long time. Yes, we try tricks to make classes as engaging as possible, using humour, an animated tone of voice to sound enthusiastic, and lots of discussion, including group work during which students are supposed to talk to their neighbours rather than listen to us. But we still have the nagging suspicion that something is not right.

Our own restlessness and physical discomfort got us thinking about whether the classroom is really a good setting for learning. We have spent a fair amount of time reflecting theoretically on the classroom, asking questions about a place we would normally take for granted. Alan wrote a book about the social relations of the classroom and the character of the educational system in a period of social change (see Sears 2003). The more we know about the classroom, the more we think our aching backs and wandering minds are trying to tell us something: the classroom does not provide a great situation for learning.

The design of the classroom assumes that the best way to learn is to sit still and listen to an expert who is lecturing from the front of the room. In larger classrooms, it is actually difficult to see and hear your fellow students if they raise questions or make points. Either they are in front of you and their backs are to you as they speak, or they are behind you and your back is to them.

The problem is that sitting and listening is not necessarily a very good way to learn. Paolo Freire (1972, 58) describes standard learning in the school system as the "banking" model of education in which students store up nuggets of wisdom passed on by their teachers. At the end of the course, students open the bottom of their piggy banks and hand back those coins in the form of correct answers on an exam.

This model assumes that the job of students is to collect knowledge and then use the amassed wealth to purchase a good grade. But when you think of the most important things you have learned in your life, they probably did not come simply through sitting passively, listening, and storing up. There might have been a classroom-like component, but that was mixed with some sort of activity. James's driving lessons, for example, included a classroom portion and a fair amount of practice driving. We doubt anyone would expect him to be able to drive a car successfully after the classroom sessions alone, even if he aced the exam. In fact, his first hands-on driving experience ended up in the ditch.

The most important learning we do always has a practice component, some form of activity. You learn to drive by driving, cook by cooking, and write by writing. Further, most of these learning situations involve interaction with others. We are helped through the practice component of learning by coaches, parents, teachers, or peers. The interaction is an important feature of the learning, not just a distraction from the sound of the teacher's voice.

Yet, as we progress through the education system, there seems to be more and more emphasis on sitting still and listening. This development is partly because our attention span expands as we mature; no one would dare try a three-hour lecture with Grade 3 students. We therefore tend to learn such sophisticated topics as social thought by listening rather than through any activity in the world. As a result, most students know theory as a set of coins they accumulate in a bank and cash out at the end of term, with nothing left behind unless there was a bit of interest (and we all know how little interest is paid on savings accounts).

Real learning is not just acquisition—it is transformation; we are changed by it. Knowledge is not a thing we pick up but a way of seeing the world and living life. Learning to cook combines bodily skills (knowing by taste how much salt to add or by feel when cream is properly whipped) with mental ones (planning a meal so that everything is done at just the right time). As you learn more about cooking, food begins to taste different. That is part of the transformation. Your approach to eating becomes more analytical as you gain the capacity to figure out the combination of herbs and spices that makes up a particular flavour sensation. We change as we learn, often in ways we do not recognize.

The banking model of education focuses primarily on acquisition rather than transformation. Schooling does, nonetheless, change us. People with more experience of formal education (for example, students in university as opposed to in Grade 10) tend to have acquired specific competencies that are very useful in the classroom. Those competencies—for example, being good at figuring out what the teacher wants you to do on an assignment—are often more important to your grade than anything else. The overt purpose of our education (to learn particular subjects and skills) is often less important than the "hidden curriculum" we are exposed to as we work our way through the school system. Terry Wotherspoon (1998, 136) says that "student school experience is shaped at least as much by everyday practices, unwritten rules and informal expectations as by the overt transmission of knowledge and skills."

David Lloyd and Paul Thomas (1998) argue that the physical design of the classroom we are now so used to was not dictated primarily by the requirements for teaching and learning particular skills or topics. It was developed in the mid-1800s by education reformers in Britain who were concerned primarily with the formation of the student as a particular kind of citizen rather than with the development of specific skills such as reading or writing.

Lloyd and Thomas (1998, 19–20) discuss the ways the relations of the classroom prepare students for their eventual place as citizens in society. In the classroom, individual students become a very specific kind of community. This community depends on the common activity of focusing attention on the teacher and following her or his directions. The students gathered in a classroom before the teacher enters are not a community but a set of individuals, some of whom are linked by ties of friendship or collegiality and others with few ties to anyone else in the room. The teacher summons the room to order as a community and regulates the social relations between the individuals gathered there.

The key relationship that defines this classroom community is hierarchical—not primarily horizontal (the relations between students, who are relatively equal in power) but vertical (relations between students and the teacher who is the power figure). The teacher is the expert and the adjudicator, operating from a supposed position of objectivity. The teacher sets the terms for participation and grants students a voice in exchange for their silence when they have not been recognized after raising their hands. This community is collectivized by shared attention to the teacher but individuated by the competitive grading system that means students pass or fail on their own.

The relationship of students to their teacher prepares them for their eventual position as citizens of the state. Citizenship is not defined primarily by horizontal relationships (with other citizens) but by vertical ones (with state authorities and institutions). The teacher is the embodiment of the idea of neutral authority or "blind justice" that the state claims to represent through policing, the judiciary, and a whole set of regulatory activities that help shape citizens with a particular set of expectations and attitudes (Sears 2003, 34).

As you look around the classroom, it is worth thinking about what the room itself is designed to teach you. Freire and others argue convincingly that the banking model teaches us little as far as course content is concerned, but they are just as persuasive when arguing that the classroom does indeed teach us a great deal about how to become self-disciplined citizens who respect, and often fear, the power of the authority figure. Just as the embodied experience of actually driving a car is an essential part of learning how to drive a car, the embodied experience of sitting obediently before the teacher in a boring, stuffy classroom is an essential part of learning to live a life of obedience. It is easy to take the classroom for granted as a space for teaching and learning because this kind of place is used in so many educational and training activities. But, as we examine this space theoretically, we step back from the obvious and ask questions about how and why it got to be this way.

WHOSE KNOWLEDGE COUNTS?

THE CLASSROOM frames a particular approach to knowledge, which is based on the assumption that the expertise is at the front of the room and the learning coming forth from the teacher is equally relevant to all of us, regardless of our backgrounds or interests. The knowledge on offer through the educational system claims to be universal and all-embracing, but, in reality, it is necessarily partial and one-sided. For example, through the educational system in Canada and the United States, we learn to see the world primarily through the eyes of Europeans and people of European ancestry. The peoples of Africa, Asia, the Americas, and Australia enter the picture most often when they are explored or conquered by European empires. They are presented as knowable only through European eyes. The cultural and scientific approaches that are taught in school can be considered Eurocentric in that they treat the specific historical experiences of peoples of European ancestry as if they tell the whole story of all of humanity (see Gordon 1995).

This Eurocentrism is so taken for granted that it is often not visible to those who practice it. It creates a deep-seated racism that often flies below the radar screen of people who are "white." As Himani Bannerji (1995, 46) writes, "Racism is not simply a set of attitudes and practices that they level towards us, their socially constructed 'other,' but it is the very principle of self-definition of European/Western societies." Every time we refer to the continent of North America and call the northern part of that Canada, we are making certain assumptions about whose land this is and how it got to be this way. The violent subjugation of Indigenous peoples and their claims to the land simply vanish in the everyday act of referring to the place in terms that are explicitly Europeanized. These kinds of assumptions are built into the subjects and disciplines we study in school.

People who are not of European ancestry often feel excluded by this way of knowing. Dionne Brand (1998, 176) investigates this exclusion as she describes her schooling in Trinidad around the time it became independent from Great Britain:

> We went to school to become people we were not, we went to school to become people we would not be ashamed of, we went to school to uplift the new Black nation, we went to school to become people who could be acceptable to the country we were seeking independence from. We went to school not to become ourselves but to get rid of ourselves.

People who are excluded from the **ways of knowing** on offer in the educational system are often left feeling that the logical conclusion of schooling is to get rid of themselves. Resistance against this feeling can be seen in the language of supporters of African-centric schools in Toronto. These schools would operate with the express purpose of giving voice to marginalized ways of knowing. During a public meeting on the issue in November 2007, one mother in attendance said, "The curriculum itself needs to address and look at areas that promote and teach our children about their culture and their history that has never been granted" (CTV 2007).

Dorothy Smith (1990, 21) writes that the academic world is built around masculinized ways of thinking that mean women can succeed only by losing their own identity: "The problem remains; we must suspend our sex and suspend our knowledge of who we are as well as who it is that is in fact speaking and of whom." She argues that the powerful institutions in our society divide knowledge into two sharply separated modes: "one located in the body and in the space it occupies and moves in, the other passing beyond it" (Smith 1990, 17). There are ways of knowing that are directly connected with our bodily experience and others that are far from it. Our knowledge of cooking, driving, hitting a baseball, or stopping a baby from crying is deeply rooted in our bodies, so much so that we often do these activities without thinking and might have trouble describing in detail what we are actually doing. On the other hand, our knowledge of social theory tends to come from books and often has very little to do with our bodily experience. The dominant division of labour means that women tend to be more engaged in caregiving than men and therefore more inclined to ways of knowing grounded in the body; for example, women may understand instinctively how the healing touch of a mother can reduce the suffering of a traumatized child.

The educational system favours the more abstract and rationalized knowledge "passing beyond" the body, a knowledge that tends to be more tied to the experiences of men than to those of women. Men tend to learn to suppress emotion and to organize their lives into separate compartments so that, for example, an illness at home does not interfere with their functioning in their jobs at the office or the factory. Women are just as capable of these things, but the dominant division of labour gives them more responsibility for caregiving that is not easily compartmentalized. A sick child or a confused elderly parent does not fit in easily with the timetable requirements of paid employment in contemporary society.

Theoretical reflection on the classroom, then, highlights features that are not obvious in everyday experience. It has been mostly the preserve of highly educated, white, upperclass men. In our view, this legacy should lead us not to shut down theoretical thinking because it is horribly contaminated by its past but to open it up. One way to achieve that is to develop the capacity for theoretical thinking, so you are learning not only theories but also how to bring new insights to your own analysis of the world around you.

Another is to open up the idea of who is a theorist. For example, Robin D.G. Kelley (2002, 154) argues that the radical black feminist movement has widened the conception of the source of theory: "It expanded the definition of who constitutes a theorist, the voice of authority speaking for black women, to include poets, blues singers, storytellers, painters, mothers, preachers, and teachers." Many people have rich insights into the way our society works, insights that are derived from their reflection on the world as they engage in their life activities rather than from theory classes in some institution of formal education.

ABSTRACTION: THE ZOOM LENS

IT IS amazing what happens when you begin to wonder about something you thought you already knew. The core of theoretical thinking is that it allows you to reframe your view of the world around you. It allows you to zoom in very close, as though looking through a microscope and seeing in detail the many kinds of activity that take place in a tiny drop of liquid that looked perfectly clear. It also provides you with the ability to pull way back, to form a broader view of the whole—like the views of the planet Earth taken from satellites that allow you to see the North and South poles at the same time.

Theoretical thinking operates as a conceptual rather than a physical zoom lens. Theories provide tools for reflecting both on the tiny processes of daily interaction that normally escape our notice and on the grand view of time and space that is well beyond our usual field of vision. We will use the term "abstraction" here to describe this zoom-lens feature of theoretical thinking.

The classroom, for example, is something you already know very well. The preceding sections of this chapter tried to get you to look at the classroom from different perspectives than you normally do. Most of us begin our reflections on the world with our own experiences and those of the people who are closest to us. We supplement this initial orientation with views of the world that we get through books, the Internet, movies, newspapers, radio, or television.

As we experience a particular situation over time, we generally begin to take it for granted. We file it in the category "already know that" or more simply "well, duh." We trust the insights that come from our experiences and use these as foundations upon which to build ever more complex understandings of the world around us. Yet serious theoretical thinking challenges us to assume that the world as presented to us in experience can be very misleading. Bertell Ollman (1993, 11) argues strongly that analysis needs to go beyond appearances:

> The problem here arises from the fact that reality is more than appearances, and that focusing exclusively on appearances, on the evidence that strikes us, immediately and directly, can be extremely misleading.

All of us face many situations in which we have no desire to probe beneath the surface and ask hard questions about the appearance of things. For example, in the novel *Three*

Junes by Julia Glass, Fenno reflects on his brother Dennis's lack of interest in probing more deeply into certain incidents: "Sometimes I wonder at Dennis's acceptance of the surface, as if the way things appear is enough for him." Yet Dennis does not accept this surface level in every area of life. He is a professional chef who is passionate about his vocation: "But I suppose that other, more virtuous mysteries consume him: how cheeses age, how meats roast, why yeast and eggs rise and collapse" (Glass 2003, 190).

Much of the time, we are simply willing to accept surface appearances, but there are some things we want to probe into deeper, to get beyond the descriptive questions (when and where) and ask the more analytical ones (how and why). We don't really care about how our computers work, but we spend a lot of time wondering about how humans learn. Others are fascinated by the intricacies of mathematical reasoning, the potential for artificial intelligence, or the development of innovative code.

Sometimes psychological reasons prevent us from opening a can of worms by asking the big questions. Other times, familiarity leads us to accept things that might seem startling or incongruent to a stranger. People with extensive experience as students and teachers in educational institutions know a great deal about the classroom and the way it operates. There is no great mystery about what goes on there. By Alan's fourth year as a university student, he went into most classes expecting to be bored and was occasionally pleasantly surprised by a really interesting teacher who got him engaged with the material.

Imagine the questions a stranger who had never taken a university or college course might ask while observing a class in session. She might stop by certain classrooms and wonder why the person at the front was reading aloud in a monotonous voice when it was patently obvious that no one was listening. She would observe certain students who tried to act like courtroom reporters by transcribing every single valuable word, while others doodled, whispered to neighbours, slept, or stared off into space. A stranger would see things in this setting that people who occupy it every day do not, just as a guest in a home might notice patterns that the inhabitants fail to identify.

Thinking Point: South-Up Maps

Drawing a map is a process of abstraction. It involves a selection indicating what's important and what's not within a particular context. If you were mapping city streets, it would make sense not to try to draw every tree in the area, as trees are irrelevant to street navigation and attempting to include them would cause trouble. Of course, if you were mapping the best places to spot birds or have a picnic in town or if you needed to know where saplings should be planted, a map including trees might be desirable. The point is that the process of abstraction is always about choosing what to leave in and what to leave out of the picture, as well as how the features of maps will be depicted in relation to each other. These choices do not happen in a vacuum. They are made from a particular standpoint that tends to be reflected in the shape of the abstraction.

A typical map of the world places the Northern Hemisphere on top and the Southern Hemisphere on the bottom. Canada, the United States, and Europe sit atop Mexico, Brazil, and Africa. But this way of representing the globe is a matter of conventional abstraction, not a fact independent of observation. There is no natural up and down in space; the abstraction is socially located. Critics of unequal power relations in global affairs have drawn attention to the way in which even our most familiar ways of representing geography privileges the countries of the North over those of the South by arranging northern nations in a superior position. The Uruguayan artist Joaquín Torres-García used the power of abstraction to raise questions about this practice by creating an "Inverted Map of South America" (Ríos n.d.). It shows the tip of the continent at the top of the map and the equator at the bottom. As you can see from the image below, south-up maps can make for a visually jarring lesson in the power of abstraction. It is important to recognize the role of social relations in shaping not only maps of space but also the conceptual frameworks ("mental maps") we use to describe and analyse society.

. The process of categorization always involves abstraction. Make a list of ten social categories often used to describe groups of people (for example, working and unemployed would be two categories). What characteristics are central to the process of abstraction, and what is left out of the picture? As a result of discussing your ten categories, do you notice any patterns in terms of what is left in and what is left out?

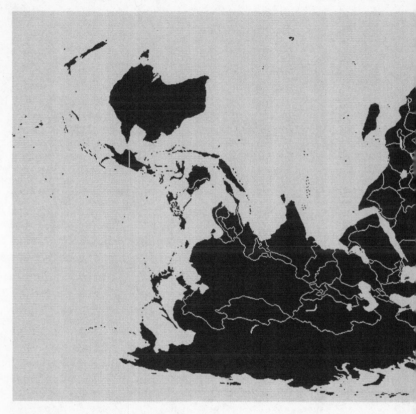

Map 4.1 Map of the World, South Up

One of the challenges of the humanities and social sciences is that they focus on the human condition and therefore ask penetrating questions about the familiar, and these questions can be accused of being rather obvious. For example, take the question "How do we know?"—the central question of the previous chapter. At first glance, it seems painfully obvious that we know something when we see it or, more precisely, when we can put a name on it such as "cat" or "dog." We are generally satisfied if something we see fits into a category we already have in our heads or if we can figure out what it is by looking it up or asking someone. We tend not to ask complicated questions about the relationship between the image we

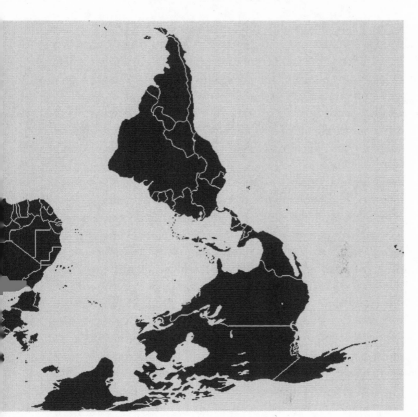

form in our brain and what is actually out there in the world. One of the aims of theoretical thinking is to help push beneath the surface, such as by examining settings that might be very familiar.

As discussed previously, for example, the classroom can be understood as a social setting structured around particular forms of inequality through a specific historical process involving institutions such as the state. That is a macroscopic view, examining the broad processes with an emphasis on the interrelation between the different aspects of a necessarily complex reality. A microscopic view, on the other hand, highlights the ways that individuals negotiate the rules of a particular setting and establish themselves in relation to others. Teachers and students work through the rules and conventions of the classroom to meet their own goals, in the process establishing a self for the setting. The self an individual constructs is bound to vary considerably with the setting: a student might be quiet and meek in the classroom and yet a loud and bold leader for the football team.

The zoom lens of abstraction, then, allows analysis to move from the microscopic, close examinations to macroscopic, grand visions. Ollman (1993, 24) examines the concept of abstraction in detail. Abstraction describes the process of framing an issue, establishing boundaries that define a discrete phenomenon within an always-interconnected reality. He begins with the simple notion that all reflection on reality requires breaking it into manageable parts (Ollman 1993, 24). People dissect reality all the time, often unconsciously. At the most basic level, we differentiate objects with our eyes in the way we focus on certain things and their surroundings. We establish foreground and background and divide our surroundings into meaningful units. This activity varies according to the character of the situation and the personality of the individual. A serious birdwatcher will look around the woods very differently than a cross-country runner racing through them. It is quite remarkable to be in a forest filled with birdwatchers who crowd around to marvel at some little speck on a branch you can't even see, let alone distinguish from a common sparrow.

As we move into the realm of theoretical thinking, we become more conscious of the ways that abstraction is employed to frame our view of reality. It is important to understand the process by which certain things have been included in the frame while others have been excluded. Ollman (1993, 40) suggests there are three dimensions to the process of abstraction: extension, level of generality, and vantage point. Extension describes the specific limits in time and space that bound a particular abstraction. The level of generality of an abstraction can range from the most specific (emphasizing the features that set a particular phenomenon apart) to the most general (emphasizing those features shared with other entities). Finally, vantage point describes the perspective built into each abstraction that necessarily views reality from a particular location.

The three dimensions of the process of abstraction will be clearer if we go back to the examination of the classroom. As an undergraduate student, the abstractions we used to reflect on the classroom tended to be (1) local, focusing on the programs and institutions we had studied in, and immediate to the period of our studies (extension = place and time); (2) very specific, focusing on the courses we had taken and the professors who had taught us (level of generality); and (3) from the perspective of relatively unmotivated undergraduates (vantage point). In contrast, when we began to write articles about education, the abstractions we used were (1) broader in time and place (extension); (2) more general, emphasizing broad similarities between classroom processes (level of generality); and (3) from the perspective of teachers with a particular set of politics (vantage point).

Everyone reading this book will have some insights into the classroom from her or his own experiences at some level. These insights necessarily involve abstractions. The challenge in theoretical thinking, as discussed at length in the previous chapter, is to be much more conscious and often more explicit about these abstractions. Do they derive from and apply to a particular time and place (extension)? To what extent do they describe only personal experience as opposed to common elements of schooling in general (level of generality)? What location framed these abstractions (vantage point)?

The same room can look very different when it is framed by a different set of abstractions. Think for a moment about the obvious difference between a teacher's experience of a classroom and a student's. The view from the front of the room with everyone looking at you and waiting for you to make things happen is quite different from that of the students who expect someone else to take charge. To add an additional dimension, imagine how the experience of that room might be different if your gender, race or ethnicity, sexuality, or social class were different. For example, as white male teachers, we learned a great deal by reading Himani Bannerji's description of her experiences as a non-white woman teaching in the classroom:

> I am an exception in the universities, not the rule. As a body type I am meant for another kind of work—but nonetheless I am in the classroom. And what is more, I am an authority. I grade and therefore I am a gatekeeper of an institution which only marginally tolerates people like us in scarcity rather than plenty. What I speak, even when not addressing gender, race and class, does not easily produce suspension of disbelief. (Bannerji 1995, 61)

Thinking Point: Framing Knowledge

There you are, sweaty and tired after a long hike up the side of a canyon, marvelling at the stunning view. Suddenly, a busload of tourists dressed for a walk down Main Street crowds around you, having driven up the heights that you scaled with your own two feet. The ultimate frustration is overhearing someone say, "It's as pretty as a postcard" or "This looks just like an ad."

The same beautiful view can summon up very different responses, depending on how the view is framed. Again, we can understand these differences in terms of (1) extension, (2) level of generality, and (3) vantage point. In terms of extension (1), the long climb up to the peak means that the view you get at the top is framed in time and space by the experience of the climb, the long haul up that offered you many visual experiences along the way. It is not a one-off, sudden, dramatic experience, as it might be if you were on a bus that just turned off the highway and presented you with an instant grand view.

The level of generality (2) might, at first, seem to be comparable, no matter which means you used to get to the top. After all, you are seeing the same sights below from exactly the same height. However, if you climbed up under your own steam, you also have some sense of the valley below and can pick out specific landmarks that you earlier saw close up. The folks on the bus see the same pretty view, but they get *only* the big picture and are unable to conjure up the same details that you can. Even at the same height, they are viewing the valley from a higher level of abstraction than you in that they are grasping only the highest level of generality. You, on the other hand, combine the mountaintop view at a high level of generality with your previous detailed close-ups at a lower level.

Finally, we get to the issue of vantage point (3). Again, everyone is looking at the valley from the same physical place, but that is not the only consideration that frames your view of it. Your experience of the view might be inflected with a particular shot of moral superiority because you climbed the mountain on your own. You have earned the view with your own sweat. That moral sense might be tempered if you realized that the people on the bus were mobility impaired and that the climb you just did would be absolutely impossible in a wheelchair, with a walker, or with arthritic joints. Your vantage point, then, depends not only on where you are looking from but also on your key assumptions about, for example, tourism and leisure activities.

The abstractions we use in social theory are similarly framed. Émile Durkheim (1966), for example, wrote the book *Suicide* in 1897. His aim was to develop a unique sociological understanding of suicide, one distinct from the psychological. He did not investigate the personal experiential factors that might lead individuals to kill themselves but rather the sociological factors that led to very different suicide rates among diverse social groups. He found that Protestants had higher suicide rates than Catholics in certain European nations and that married people with children had lower suicide rates than single people or childless married couples. He concluded that higher suicide rates were connected to more individualistic lifestyles and less intensive social cohesion, a phenomenon that produced *anomie*, or normlessness.

The concept of anomie is framed in very specific ways in Durkheim's work. It is (1) located in time and space (extension), as it is not a universal human condition but a phenomenon peculiar to industrialized societies that have emerged over the past 200 years. Earlier forms of social organization did not produce anomie in this sense, and it is at least hypothetically possible that a very different society in the future might not either.

Anomie is also (2) at quite a high level of generality. It is not a characteristic of individuals (this child is more anomic than that one) but of social groups in specific situations. It is, therefore, not necessarily obvious at the level of day-to-day experience. Protestants in Durkheim's time might not have felt more anomic than Catholics, nor did they appear so in any obvious way to an immediate observer. It was only at the level of the statistical comparison of suicide rates that these differences were visible. That this finding was observable at a high level of generality does not make it any less true or important, but it does mean that the phenomenon of anomie needs to be sought out and investigated in the right places.

Finally, anomie is framed by Durkheim's vantage point (3) on his world. He was worried about the upheaval that seemed to be characteristic of the emerging industrialized society of the 1800s. The arrival of industrial society in France, Durkheim's own country, had produced a succession of insurgent uprisings and revolutions. According to Durkheim, the great challenge for sociology as a discipline was to overcome this turmoil by helping to identify the kinds of shared values that might produce a more sustainable industrial society. Durkheim himself favoured neither further revolutionary change nor turning back the clock to the good old days. The old values that had sustained order in previous times (such as traditional religions) were outmoded, and social peace depended on the development of new values compatible with an industrial society. Every time we use the term anomie, it bears the weight of those founding assumptions.

Any individual will find certain abstractions easy to digest and others hard to take. The "suspension of disbelief" generally happens when we trust the source and do not challenge its analysis. Someone who offers up abstractions that do not fit easily with the ones students have assimilated over time is unlikely to be received with the "suspension of disbelief" and more likely to be challenged. A challenge is particularly likely when the individual offering up the abstraction does not fit with the (white, male) model of authority that tends to apply in this society. Reading Bannerji's words made us reflect on how our perceptions of the classroom are framed by our experiences as white male instructors who get the benefit of the doubt.

A good course in theoretical thinking will introduce you to some viewpoints that you agree with and others that you do not. Some things you read might clarify insights you have had for a long time while others will seem totally impossible to understand. The person beside you might see them in exactly the opposite way. The aim of this discussion is not to persuade you to adopt a particular view of the classroom but to remind you that you already have one and might benefit from becoming more conscious of it. The more you are aware of the abstractions that frame your own thinking, the more you will be able to handle the various theories that are used in the social sciences. And, in a cyclical fashion, the greater your grasp on a range of formal theories, the more you will be able to sharpen your own perspective on the classroom and beyond.

Thinking Point: Contrasting Maps

This chapter uses the analysis of the classroom in formal educational settings to ground a discussion of the way key abstractions frame our theoretical understanding of a setting. The particular analysis of the classroom presented here is based on certain abstractions, assumptions about the way the educational system works and how it fits into the broader society. These assumptions are hotly debated in the realm of social theory.

Thus far in this chapter, the discussion of education has been founded on the premises of conflict theory, which presumes that the current society is based on inequalities that create conflicts and can only be overcome through significant social change. The education system contributes to the perpetuation of this unjust social order by preparing people to accept their eventual place either as rulers or subordinates.

Theoretical discussion of the education system is informed by assumptions about the way society works and how things change. As a way of getting better at doing this sort of analysis on your own, read the short description of the education system below and note the ways in which its core assumptions contrast with the conflict model. You may notice right away that this framework for understanding schooling, this "map" of the education system, aligns well with the social order model. The challenge is to trace back specific statements about the education system to the core assumptions of the social order perspective. Because this description is a condensed summary, it can seem too neat and tidy. But, in fact, it is rooted in important assumptions that governments and educators have used to shape education policy over centuries:

A Social Order Perspective: School as Preparation for Industrial Society

Schooling is the best way for people in industrial societies to socialize their children. It provides the young with the skills, values, and drives required to succeed in a complex and rapidly changing world. Mass public schooling developed only with the rise of modern industrial society during the 1800s. Since then, the basic pattern has been one of increased participation, so that more people receive more years of schooling in each successive generation.

The socialization of the young becomes more specialized in an industrial society, where individuals require a wide range of skills and aptitudes to negotiate the challenges of everyday life. Traditionally, children learned by doing, working, and playing alongside their kin and other members of their communities. These traditional child-rearing methods were no longer adequate with the rise of an industrial society, when it became necessary to rear individuals who could read and write, add and subtract, vote, search for jobs, move away to seek work as necessary, be patriotic, and nurture the next generation with very limited external support. People need a much higher level of preparation for life in a modern industrial society than was required in simpler traditional ones.

The increased participation in education addresses this issue. Further, the increased emphasis on schooling can be taken as the marker of a more democratic society in which positions of authority are increasingly gained on the basis of *achievement*, the individual accomplishments that qualify someone for power, as opposed to *ascription*, being born into it. Now you need to be properly qualified for a job, by education and experience, rather than simply inheriting it from a parent. Increased educational attainment is one measure of a more just society.

Before moving on to the next chapter, spend a few minutes reflecting on precisely how this perspective fits with the social order model. Try to be methodical in your approach. For example, you might want to go back to the chart in Chapter 2 and reacquaint yourself with the key premises of the various theoretical perspectives. Now go through the description again, this time writing the letter "S" in the margin wherever you spot an idea that aligns with the social order model's premises. It might be useful to conclude by writing a short paragraph or explaining to a classmate what it is, specifically, about the argument that would lead you to place it in the social order camp.

When you first encounter an argument in assigned readings or in debates with friends or online conversations, it can be useful to do a quick gut-level check with yourself about what theoretical perspective it reminds you of. However, methodical inquiry requires not only being able to label arguments as being consistent with one or another theory but being able to trace individual elements of the argument to the core premises of theoretical models.

5

*The Real World: Making
Sense of Perceptions*

Each social theory provides us with a vision of what is
realistic in the context of the world we inhabit. This chapter
explores the idea of reality and its place in social theory.

Reality seems like something outside us, the external world
independent of our thoughts. Yet social theories such as **phenomenology**, which we explore in this chapter, remind us that
we produce the outside world by filtering and organizing the
things we see, hear, smell, taste, and feel. We sort things into
categories all the time, without thinking about it. We see an
animal and make it a cat or a dog, determine if it is friendly
or fierce, beautiful or ugly, smart or dumb, all before we have
really thought about it.

A large chunk of this chapter is designed to problematize
the whole idea of reality, to make it a challenge we need to
think about rather than something obvious. The final sections
deal with the idea of realism in the context of society and with
postmodern challenges to the assumption that a "real" world
exists in the first place. What is realistic in any given situation is a matter of debate. Different theoretical perspectives
provide a very different read on what is or is not realistic.

THE REAL WORLD AND THE IVORY TOWER

Students often worry about the relationship between
the things they learn in their courses and the real world
out there. Unless you go on to graduate school, it is quite
unlikely that you will ever again hear the names of many of
the writers you study in a theory class. So why do you need
to know them now?

In this chapter, we will try to convince you that theoretical reflection can help prepare you for the real world by encouraging you to ask what makes things "real." At first glance, the answer is, of course, dead obvious. You know something is real when you can touch it, see it, smell it, taste it, or hear it. In other words, we associate reality with empirical data gathered through our five senses. However, the theoretical perspective of phenomenology, introduced below, raises important questions about our relationship with the apparently obvious reality around us. Because phenomenology is dedicated to studying the role of perception in making the world meaningful, you are likely to note similarities between the phenomenological theories discussed in this chapter and the "interpretive" theory of knowledge introduced in Chapter 3. Throughout this chapter, you're encouraged to think about the ways phenomenology raises questions about your everyday perceptions.

At any given moment, our senses are bombarded by an overwhelming amount of information. This is obvious on the crowded streets of a city you are not familiar with—the pounding traffic sounds, the push and shove of people on the crowded sidewalk, the smells of exhaust or exotic spices or fast food, the sight of towering buildings or temporary-looking shacks, and the movement everywhere. Even in a quiet library when you are trying to study, the whisper of someone a few tables over, the jingling of change in a pocket, or the flicker of a failing fluorescent light can be distracting.

We are not simply taking in all this information and storing it, like a gigantic video camera. A massive process of selection and organization goes on in our bodies and minds. John Berger (1972, 8–9) describes this process: "We only see what we look at. To look is an act of choice. . . . Our vision is continually active, continually moving, continually holding things in a circle around itself, constituting what is present to us as we are." Indeed, all of our senses are active, not passive, working on the world out there and not simply taking it in.

The process does not end there, for an important organizing process occurs as our senses take the information in.

We assimilate new experiences by connecting them to previous ones, classifying them as similar or dissimilar (e.g., the frogs' legs do or do not taste like chicken). The notion of reality quickly becomes more complicated as we reflect on it theoretically.

THE REAL AND THE IMAGINARY

CANADIAN WRITER Margaret Atwood argues that her own sense of reality was shaped in part by her childhood experience of spending time remote from her extended family at the research station in northern Québec where her father worked: "none of my relatives were people I could actually see, my own grandmothers were no more and no less mythological than Little Red Riding Hood's grandmother." Consequently, she explains, she grew up as an avid reader who found little to distinguish between the fictional worlds of the books she read and the distant worlds inhabited by her relatives. In these circumstances, she developed a mindset that equipped her well to be a writer: "the inability to distinguish between the real and the imagined, or rather the attitude that what we consider real is also imagined" (Atwood 2000, 7).

"What we consider real is also imagined": Margaret Atwood has given us a rather elegant statement of the more complex version of reality we are exploring here. The real world and the world of the imagination are not separate and opposed but are deeply interconnected. This is not to deny that there is a real world out there—although, as will become very clear when we examine postmodern theory, the question of whether reality exists is certainly a topic of considerable debate among social theorists. The real world might be out there, but you, your friends, and people on the other side of the world have access to it only through the actions of our own minds and bodies. We need to touch it, taste it, see it, smell it, or hear it. These sensations are organized in our thoughts according to classification schemes of which we are seldom directly aware.

If we did not organize our thoughts, we would be overwhelmed by sensations. We can only cope with the tremendous overload of sense data we receive every second by filtering out most of it and focusing selectively. We are not even aware of this filtering process most of the time; we simply accept that some noise is background (the foot-tapping of the person sitting beside you) and other noise is foreground (the sweet tone of your professor's voice).

The presence of this filtering process becomes most obvious when we contrast it with the experience of autistic people, who often have great difficulty organizing sense data. Dr. Temple Grandin is a person living with autism who used her powerful visual imagination to become a professor and designer despite her difficulties with written communication and in certain interpersonal settings. In her book, she describes the ways that ordinary sense experiences overwhelmed her. As a child, she could not bear to be touched: "It was like a great, all-engulfing tidal wave of stimulation, and I reacted like a wild animal. Being touched triggered flight; it flipped my circuit breaker" (Grandin 1995, 62).

Grandin also reports great difficulty handling sounds in the environment. Loud noises cause pain "like a dentist's drill hitting a nerve." Minor background noises distract her: "I still have problems with losing my train of thought when distracting noises occur. If a pager goes off when I am giving a lecture, it fully captures my attention and I completely forget what I was talking about." She describes the overall effect: "My ears are like microphones picking up all sounds with equal intensity" (Grandin 1995, 67–68).

Autism, then, can have the effect of flattening the sensory landscape, so that every sensation demands equal attention. In contrast, people who are not autistic are generally able to sort highlights from background. Consciousness is the process through which we organize the tidal wave of sensations into meaningful units of reality. Our environment would be an incomprehensible array of sensations were it not for our facility for consciousness, which allows us to make sense of the world actively.

It is through consciousness that we organize the sensations that bombard us. It is only through consciousness, for example, that a particular set of sensations—the barking sound, the feel of the tongue, the smell of wet fur, the look of four legs, and a particular profile—becomes a dog. As the influential phenomenologist Alfred Schutz (1978, 266) writes,

> We do not experience the world as a sum of sense data, nor as an aggregate of individual things isolated from and standing in no relation to one another. We do not see coloured spots and contours, but rather mountains, trees, animals, in particular birds, fish, dogs, etc.

Phenomenology is the theoretical school that focuses on the examination of consciousness. Jeffrey Alexander (1987, 241) describes its central premise: "reality is structured by perception. Even the things whose objectivity we normally take for granted are 'there' for us only because we make them, or take them to be so." Phenomenology studies the ways our own consciousness structures our understanding of reality in processes we do not often recognize. Driven by the interpretivist approach to inquiry discussed in Chapter 3, phenomenology examines the role that consciousness plays in constructing reality.

In our everyday lives, we rely on the core assumption that the world around us is made up of objects that exist outside of our minds and are independent of us. An object is defined in the *New Oxford Dictionary* as "a material thing that can be seen and touched." People can only see or touch things that are outside their own mind. The dictionary adds a technical definition from the field of philosophy, "a thing external to the thinking mind or subject" (Oxford 2001, 1277).

When Alan first wrote the previous paragraph, he tasted tea, heard a cat meow, felt the breeze from a fan, saw a dictionary on his desk, and smelled the fresh-cut grass in his neighbour's yard. In his experience, each of these sensations seemed to emanate from the objects themselves; in other words, he felt that his senses simply captured a bit of the reality around him. Tea has a particular flavour, for example, and his taste buds did their job by sensing that and sending a message to the brain. He assumed the taste of tea to be a property of that object, end of story.

Phenomenology challenges us not to leave the story there. The sensations we think of as properties of the objects around us are, in fact, products of our own consciousness. We don't have to deny the existence of the external world to think this way; rather, we understand that our access to this world is always mediated by our consciousness. The goal of phenomenology is to make us aware of our own role in the making of the real world that seems to exist beyond us.

Consciousness works primarily through a process of typification, sorting sensations into a series of types or categories based on similarity to previous experiences (Schutz 1978, 269). This sorting requires that our recollections of our own past are organized in an orderly fashion, as in a good filing system. New experiences are assimilated into existing categories in this system, just as any new item in a filing system gets put somewhere. If you had to open a new file for every single item that came along, the system would be useless. Similarly, if you crammed every item into one folder, you would have gained no organizational edge. The aim in filing is to develop a set of categories that enables you to identify the similarities that will lead to grouping items while at the same time noting the key differences that require separate headings. We similarly organize our sensations, though often without reflecting on the process.

Schutz (1967, 81) describes this process: "With every moment of conscious life a new item is filed away in this vast storehouse." Confronting a new situation, people retrieve a similar situation as a reference point. You wait for a call from a potential employer, and your consciousness reminds you of how it felt to sit by the phone hoping for that much-wanted call for a follow-up after a great first date. You access a whole set of feelings, behaviours, and information.

We organize our experiences around key principles that inform the whole system of categorization. Most important, we use concepts of time and space to organize our experiences into meaningful categories. Peter Berger and Thomas Luckmann (1967, 22) argue that we understand the world relative to the "here" of our bodies and the "now" of our present: "This means that I experience everyday life in terms of differing degrees of closeness and remoteness, both spatially and temporally." We sort objects around us into near and far and therefore are not shocked that people who are farther away look smaller. Of course, the first time you go up a very tall building and see people scurrying at an ant-like scale below, it can be pretty startling. Your senses quickly adapt, though, and you take for granted that those tiny specks below are people the same size you are.

Thus far, we have described consciousness in a very individualistic way, emphasizing the way each of us develops the capacity to organize our experiences in a highly orderly fashion. Yet, at the most obvious level, these categorization schemes are shared. My category "dog" and yours are probably quite similar, though we might get a very different image in our heads when the word is mentioned. Shown a picture of an animal, we are likely to agree about whether it is a dog, cat, or mouse.

Consciousness is social, then, with a serious shared element to our categorization schemes even though we have no direct access to the thoughts in each other's heads. Thus we must assume, but can never know, that others share the same kind of consciousness that we have. The nightly news is a good example of these assumptions at work in our everyday lives. In order for the news to make sense to the millions of viewers sitting in front of their television sets each night, newscasters must act upon many widely held, but unstated, assumptions about what qualifies as news, what a legitimate news story looks like, how news should be reported, how a newscast should be organized, and so on. This kind of unconscious collective assumption is central not only to the work of journalists and the mass viewing public but also to our face-to-face conversations. When Alan and I interact, I take for granted that he "is conscious, and his stream of consciousness is temporal in character, exhibiting the same basic form as mine" (Schutz 1967, 98). All of us can only understand others through **intersubjectivity**, interacting with the other on the assumption that she or he sees the world pretty much as we do.

Pet owners display intersubjectivity when they assume that their dog possesses a consciousness like their own: "Poor Fluffy. She misses me so much because I've been away all day doing my stupid job. Come here, girl, I'll make it better." Dogs are social animals, and they probably have missed you, but if they could talk, they would probably not express the thoughts you impute to them.

The tricky thing about consciousness is that it makes things seem real and outside of the head of the individual. The role of our own perceptions is relatively invisible to us. The categories do seem to exist out there, and we assume that what we are getting are little units of reality captured as if on videotape and stored in our memories. In the language of phenomenology, this stance of accepting the reality of the external world is referred to as the "natural attitude." Schutz (1978, 257) explains: "in this attitude the existence of the life-world and the typicality of its contents are accepted as unquestionably given until further notice."

In the natural attitude, then, the activities of our own consciousness in organizing the world around us are invisible to us because we assume that the characteristics we assign to each object are inherent properties of the thing itself. We assume, for example, that chocolate tastes good and spinach does not. Nothing simply tastes good, however, without an interpretive process through which we organize our sensations.

Alan used to hate the taste of beer, and his social life was a disaster. One summer, he taught himself to tolerate it so he could go out drinking and share pitchers of draft with friends. At first, he had to treat beer like a medicine, forcing it down with a handful of potato chips for a more pleasurable taste sensation. He grew to love the taste of beer and developed quite a picky palate with a preference for the more flavourful brews. He even grew to like the room-temperature draft beers served in pubs in England that made some of his fellow North Americans moan. A flavour that had once been very off-putting became so desirable that he sought out stronger forms of it. James's taste in beer is very different from Alan's, tending more to the root beer side of the family.

Beer, then, does not inherently taste good or bad. Alan taught himself to like beer through a process that included his own sensory experiences and interchange with others. People can learn to like flavours that at first seem repulsive. If beer tastes good to Alan, that is because he has organized the system in his head so that beer gets filed under "yummy." But when he cracks open a cold beer on a hot summer day after a long hike, it hits the spot, without any interpretive effort on his part. People attribute characteristics that they assign to objects around them, a process that goes through each person's individual consciousness.

Consciousness is very difficult to study because it disguises itself in the act of making the world seem real. The first step in any phenomenological investigation, then, must be to render consciousness visible. This is done through bracketing, which requires that we direct our attention away from the things on the outside and focus on our own process of making sense by organizing and classifying. As Schutz (1967, 37) writes, phenomenology involves a commitment to "attend only to . . . conscious experiences": "It is only after I . . . turn away from the world of objects . . . and direct my gaze at my inner stream of consciousness . . . that I become aware of this process of constitution." Schutz is arguing here that we only become aware of the way we actively create the world we see when we turn our attention to the work of our own consciousness. Phenomenology insists that we attend to our own role in structuring reality.

Pain, for example, seems like a simple objective phenomenon. We all take for granted that some things hurt and others do not, and we know pain when we feel it. But the theory of phenomenology urges us to go further. Serious athletes derive great pleasure out of doing things that cause pain. Our friend Peter is training for the New York Marathon, and we do not understand why he chooses to suffer. Alan knows someone with an aunt who could take anything out of the hot oven with her bare hands, never using pot holders. The authors of this book once attended a concert and left with one remarking on how interesting the music was and the other in pain from what he'd heard. In fact, James questioned whether the sounds coming from the vocal performers could be considered "music" at all. Although we did not think about it this way in the moment, we were locked in a dispute over the best way to classify sounds. James's brother has stacks of piercings and streams of tattoos, yet James faints at the sight of a needle.

There is no clear line between pain and pleasure. It is only through our consciousness that we organize sensations into these categories. Bracketing requires that we open up the question of how and why we categorize some things in a particular way while others view them differently. The next time something smells good or bad, stop to ask yourself why you think that. The smell of charred wood can bring to mind the romance of a campfire or the horrors of a burned-down family home. Neither image is a property of the thing itself.

Bracketing is a real challenge; it means going against the assumptions that serve us well and make sense of our everyday life. Berger and Luckmann (1967, 23) describe this in powerful terms:

> The reality of everyday life is taken for granted as reality. . . . I *know* that it is real. While I am capable of engaging in doubt about its reality, I am obliged to suspend such doubt as I routinely exist in everyday life. This suspension of doubt is so firm that to abandon it . . . I have to make an extreme transition.

Phenomenology invites us to make this extreme transition. Not surprisingly, many students reject this invitation, assuming it is a typical academic waste of time to ask probing questions about the obvious. Yet it is possible to gain powerful insights by bracketing, by casting doubt on the obvious. There is a great deal to learn about the simplest of our everyday interactions. For example, why does a particular piece of music sound great to you and horrible to another? The phenomenological approach leads you to attend to how your ear has been trained to listen to music in very specific ways to appreciate certain sounds and dislike others.

Ethnomethodology is a wing of phenomenological theory that focuses on the process through which social norms are integrated into consciousness. This integration is a more complicated process than it first appears to be. People generally assume that they are rule-abiding, even if, in practice, that requires a very broad interpretation of the rule. We need to be more aware of the ways we stretch the rules to cover particular situations. For example, many of us subscribe to the rule that we should tell the truth. Yet even people who would see themselves as honest will not always tell the truth when they are asked, "Does this shirt look good on me?" We do not want to be hurtful and therefore do not tell the truth in particular situations. Our consciousness allows us to reconcile our self-image as rule-abiding with everyday practices of transgression that redefine the rules.

Harold Garfinkel (1967), one of the developers of ethnomethodology, has established a practical approach to bracketing that he calls "breeching experiments." These involve practical exercises that disrupt people's everyday lives and make them more aware of the taken-for-granted assumptions that shape their existence. These "breeching experiments" require that participants perform minor disruptions that make the implicit assumptions in a situation clear. For example, in everyday conversation we do not expect a real response to the question "How are you?" Try answering with a list of ailments and complaints—"My stomach is a bit off, I've been depressed since September, and my hæmorrhoids are acting up"—and watch the other person squirm.

It is quite easy through disruption to uncover the hidden assumptions that govern personal space, conversation, eye contact with strangers, and overhearing. If there are any lingering doubts about the power of these assumptions, try standing toe-to-toe with a stranger on an elevator or relax by lying on the floor after a meal in a crowded restaurant. You will quickly see that the seemingly free and spontaneous nature of everyday life is, in fact, heavily restricted by a complex framework of unwritten social rules. Our consciousness allows us to take for granted a whole series of behaviours and actions that might otherwise appear quite outlandish. For example, public cellphone use on a bus or a train often depends on the shared understanding that no one else is listening, even if those around the speaker have no choice but to hear every word. Breeching experiments require that people speak up and join in the conversation, challenging the tacit agreement that everyone pretend this public activity is going on in private.

Thinking Point: Bracketing and Breeching Experiments

Bracketing is the commitment to looking at the world through new eyes, putting aside the interpretive process we normally use to frame reality in our consciousness. If someone waves a hand at you, you should put aside the assumption that you know what that person is doing and ask instead what it means. This is a philosophical approach to the world, one that is admittedly rather difficult to put into practice as we are so used to the world as framed by consciousness that it is almost impossible to know where the reality outside us ends and our own interpretive process begins.

The practice of meditation gives a bit of insight into bracketing. In meditation, you attempt to set aside all the content of your thoughts to reflect on thought itself. For example, you can concentrate on your own relaxed breathing or a repeated chant or the flickering of a candle with such intensity that your mind is emptied of its everyday clutter. You escape from thinking about term papers, bills, social activities for the coming weekend, or your job. Instead, you float freely in a realm of pure mind, cleansed of all particular thoughts.

There are certain parallels between the opening up of the mind through meditation and the process of bracketing as discussed in phenomenology. We are always conscious of something, and, through bracketing, we attempt to set aside the thing we are conscious of to explore consciousness itself. There is a self-reflexive character to this activity, much as there is to meditation.

Breeching experiments as proposed by ethnomethodologists provide a different approach to exposing consciousness, disrupting settings to expose the ways we act on the basis of taken-for-granted assumptions about the rules that govern a given situation. It is as simple as picking up the ringing telephone and saying nothing or moving just a bit farther away from someone than you normally would in a conversation. You begin to detect a whole set of precise rules that govern personal space, conversation, and, in fact, all of our interpersonal activities.

Finally, you will detect the complex process through which we stretch the rules to cover our own behaviour. Watch, for example, as a man who thinks of himself as polite reacts to a homeless woman on the street who asks for money or a light or even the time. Suddenly, all the basic rules of polite behaviour are off. There is no eye contact, and the homeless person is aggressively ignored whatever she is saying. Somehow, there is an interpretation of the politeness rule, perhaps an exemption on the basis that the homeless person poses a threat or is categorized as drunk or is a public nuisance not worthy of attention. Yet there is probably no evidence of a threat or drunkenness or even inconvenience. After all, a smile and a word in passing take no time.

Breeching experiments can be a really interesting way to figure out how we apply rules without thinking in social situations. At some level, hidden-camera television shows are a kind of breeching experiment, often conducted just for laughs. Television shows are not bound by the same ethical considerations that shape academic research. If you are interested in running off to begin breeching experiments, remember that the first consideration must be that you do no harm to others, whether physical, emotional, or social. With that in mind, what might your breeching experiments look like? What routine or "normal" activity might you choose to disrupt, and how? What do you think would be the results of your experiments, and what might be learned from them?

PHENOMENOLOGY AND INEQUALITY

THE PHENOMENOLOGICAL approach to the social construction of our everyday lives can be very helpful in understanding how practices of oppression are highly visible to those who face discrimination yet are not perceived by those who are exhibiting prejudice. The key axes of consciousness often include categories of race, sexuality, gender, and social class that are simply taken for granted.

The comedy show "Saturday Night Live" had a long-running skit that explored the phenomenology of gender. The character named "Pat" was hard to place as either a man or a woman. The other characters spent their time during these skits trying to label Pat as male or female. The instant categorization of people as male or female, with a whole set of expectations attached to the label, is an important part of our cultural repertoire. People are sometimes quite upset when they find out this classification is wrong. In the novel *Dead Souls* by Ian Rankin (1999, 475–76), Nicky is a transgendered person, biologically a man who appears as a woman. Nicky's sister describes what happened during a party on a boat, when Nicky picked up a guy named Damon:

> Nicky had his head on Damon's shoulder, and just for a moment our eyes met . . . and he looked so happy.
>
> But a drunk named Alfie interfered.
>
> Alfie was as drunk as I've ever seen him. For a joke, he leaned over and snatched Nicky's wig. . . . And Damon just stood there, like he was thunderstruck. He looked . . . it seemed rather hilarious at the time. His face was a picture. Then he ran for the stairs.
>
> Nicky ran after him, pursued by his sister.
>
> By the time I came up on deck, this Damon person had Nicky down on the ground. He was strangling the life out of him, and at the same time thumping his head against the deck.

Damon, then, had a great deal invested in the categorization of Nicky as a woman rather than as a man. Once the wig was snatched and Nicky appeared as a man, Damon responded violently. A similar situation is depicted in the 1999 movie *Boys Don't Cry*, but here the story depicts the real life ordeal of Brandon Teena, a transgendered man who was abused and eventually murdered because of his identity. Transgendered people frequently face violence and harsh discrimination in contemporary Western society where those who upset people's gender categorization may be punished with brutality.

Phenomenological theory has tended to spend insufficient time examining the ways that consciousness is gendered, although the theory offers potentially valuable tools for understanding the process through which gendered expectations are imposed in our everyday lives (see Levesque-Lopman 1988). Gender is one of the first things we tend to see in other human beings, and, in those cases where it is not obvious, such as a baby, parents will often go to great lengths with blue and pink outfits to make sure gender is visible.

The visible signs associated with "race" (skin colour, eye shape, hair texture) also tend to register very quickly in the consciousness of contemporary North Americans. Even those "white" people who are not overtly racist quickly categorize others according to **racialized** criteria. Frantz Fanon (1967) was a person of colour raised in the former French colony of Martinique where the educational system taught him he was French. However, when he moved to France to pursue further studies, he was reminded all the time that he was black. White people always saw his skin colour and categorized him on that basis. Fanon (1967, 116) writes the following about his experiences upon entering a room: "I feel, I see in those white faces that it is not a new man who has come in, but a new kind of man, a new genus. Why, it's a Negro!"

Consciousness, then, is highly racialized and gendered. In other words, it is an active part of the "process whereby groups are given racial [and gender] markings depending on changing socio-political and economic conditions, rather than biology" (Mehta 2009, 8). It is also highly attuned to markers of sexuality and social class. Even when we stop saying overtly racist, sexist, and homophobic things, in this unequal society, we generally face a complex secondary process of dealing with the ways categories of class, gender, race and ethnicity, and sexuality frame our consciousness at levels of which we are not aware. It is not natural to sort people on first sight into these categories; it is the product of a society in which the relations of gender, race and ethnicity, sexuality, and social class are very important. Even people who think they practice "colour-blind" interaction, for example, often have a highly racialized consciousness. Thus, phenomenology provides us with valuable tools for understanding the way our real world is structured.

Thinking Point: Racial Profiling

The issue of racial profiling by police, airport security, and border guards is an important example of racialized consciousness. Racial profiling means that people get targeted on the basis of perceived membership in a group associated with particular stereotypes rather than because of anything they have done. A young black man might get stopped by police simply for walking in a particular area. Anti-racist and human rights activists have complained about racial profiling by police for a long time. The issue has been even more prominent in the reaction to 9/11. Some governments and policing agencies have sought to make racial profiling official policy rather than an unofficial practice.

Racial profiling works on an everyday level when a police officer or border guard identifies someone as a potential problem on the basis of characteristics such as skin colour, hair, or style of dress. The individual officers may not be aware of the criteria they are using to define a certain person as a potential troublemaker or how their classification system has developed on the basis of personal experiences and prejudices, conversations with other security officials, media coverage, statements by politicians, or, at times, explicit departmental directives.

The profiling of people of North African, Middle Eastern, or South Asian backgrounds and those perceived as religiously Islamic has been a human rights issue for a long time. It has sharply intensified since 9/11. Alarm bells are now set off inside security officials' heads whenever they see certain items of clothing or particular racialized characteristics. They may not even be aware of the extent to which this profiling is happening, as consciousness works beneath the radar as taken-for-granted activities rather than deliberate choices. As a result, people belonging to certain groups find themselves singled out for attention every time they come into contact with the security apparatus, while others are waved through with minimal scrutiny.

The past decade has seen numerous cases in which Canadian citizens from Middle Eastern and North African backgrounds have been unlawfully detained and tortured outside Canada with the permission of the Canadian government. It is no coincidence but the product of systemic racial profiling that these cases have all involved the mistreatment of racialized citizens. Between May and August 2009, Suaad Hagi Mohamud was detained in Kenya because officials there claimed that she did not appear to be the same woman depicted in her Canadian passport. Despite her pleas for help to the Canadian government, it took nearly four months and a DNA test to prove that she was indeed who she said she was. This is not the first time that questions have been raised about differences between passport photographs and people's appearance, but it is virtually impossible to imagine Mohamud's ordeal being experienced by a white male Canadian citizen. Deep-seated prejudices about marginalized groups are directly connected to the unequal treatment of racialized people.

DREAMS AND THE
CONSTRUCTION OF REALITY

THERE ARE certain moments in the average day when we are more likely to become aware of the workings of our consciousness. One of these is when we wake up from slumber, whether from a night's sleep or from a nap. At least some of the time, we experience an overlap between our dreams and our waking consciousness. The alarm clock enters into the dream, or we expect to find a character from the dream in the room with us when we wake.

All of us perform our own daily breeching experiments when we wake up from a deep sleep. Marcel Proust brilliantly described this process of coming to consciousness in his novel *Swann's Way*:

> But for me it was enough if, in my own bed, my sleep was so heavy as completely to relax my consciousness; for then I lost all sense of the place in which I had gone to sleep, and when I awoke at midnight, not knowing where I was, I could not be sure at first who I was. (Proust 1999, 3)

Consciousness, then, helps us to locate ourselves in the world. Without that, we do not know ourselves. The world then becomes unfixed:

> Perhaps the immobility of the things that surround us is forced upon them by our conviction that they are themselves, and not anything else, and by the immobility of our conceptions of them. For it always happened that when I awoke like this, and my mind struggled in an unsuccessful attempt to discover where I was, everything would be moving round me through the darkness: things, places, years. (Proust 1999, 4)

Things that we normally think of as fixed may seem fluid as we wake up. This is a reminder that the solidity of things is not given by the outside world but constructed in our consciousness.

Walter Benjamin invites us to go one step further and inquire whether our everyday consciousness does actually represent a state of being awake. He raises the possibility that, in contemporary capitalist societies, we live our daily lives in shared dreamworlds. As Benjamin (1999, 389) writes, "The situation of consciousness as patterned and checkered by sleep and waking need only be transferred from the individual to the collective." This is a provocative notion—that we collectively sleepwalk through our daily lives, dreaming of the better life that will come when we win the lottery, buy the right clothes, use the newest cleansers, or drive the coolest cars. The dreamworld is shared and therefore invisible to each of us as individuals.

If we share a collective dreamworld, as Benjamin argues, then awakening would be a collective and not just an individual activity. Following Benjamin's argument, then, we could say that people tend to wake themselves up collectively when they enter into activism as a movement. They begin to see things clearly that were never so obvious before. Things that had seemed to be outside of their control, rather like the weather, suddenly seem to be products of human activity that they can challenge. So often, the news can seem just like the weather report—storms are blowing in, and there is nothing you can do about it except buy an umbrella. In his argument that the invention of the telegraph in the late 1800s is largely to blame for today's "information glut," Neil Postman (1985, 68) wrote that "most of our daily news is inert, consisting of information that gives us something to talk about but cannot lead to any meaningful action." But, as people collectively awaken from the dream that Benjamin describes, the news can become a challenge to act.

Benjamin's idea of collective dreaming is a big challenge to our everyday assumptions about reality. We might think that everything is real when we are awake and walking through the mall. Walter Benjamin, however, invites us to consider the possibility that we are sleepwalking through a collective dream state in which we imagine that these consumer goods will actually deliver us from the humdrum existence of our daily lives.

REALITY? GET REAL!

PHENOMENOLOGICAL THEORIES of reality certainly pose a radical challenge to people who downplay the role of perception in constructing how reality is approached, categorized, and, ultimately, comprehended. However, the phenomenological tradition discussed in this chapter is by no means the most radical interpretation of what reality is or of how it is accessed by humans. Postmodern theory, introduced in Chapter 2, raises questions about whether reality exists at all.

If this is your first time encountering this idea, it may strike you as being completely absurd. Reality doesn't exist? Then who is this person sitting beside me on the bus? And why can't I go five seconds without thinking about the mosquito bite on my knee? And where did that ten-dollar bill go that went missing from my dresser last week? That our everyday lives appear to confirm so clearly that reality *does indeed* exist should prepare us for the fact that, whatever it is that postmodernists are getting at when they say that there's no such thing as reality, it definitely isn't going to be a simple argument.

Make no mistake: although postmodern theory can be bold and thought-provoking, it tends also to be complex, confusing, and contradictory. The writing of postmodernists is often criticized for being riddled with difficult language or academic jargon, and for proposing ideas that run against anything remotely resembling common sense. One particularly striking example of the characteristically absurdist logic of postmodernism is found in the title of Jean Baudrillard's 1995 book, *The Gulf War Did Not Take Place*. The observation that postmodern theory does not lend itself to easy understanding has been made not only by critics of postmodernism but also by postmodern theorists such as Baudrillard, Jacques Derrida, and Gayatri Spivak, who argue that their fragmentary and convoluted writing style is an essential feature of their theoretical perspective. In other words, some postmodernists would say that their style must appear as a patchwork of random, unconventional ideas and unfamiliar language because, no matter how hard some authors have tried to tell the world as it is, clarity and truth are hopeless goals. So, if the postmodern theory that you're reading in school strikes you as more than a little difficult to understand, rest assured that you're not alone. In fact, your confusion might even be a sign that you're on to something!

Postmodern theory's signature brashness and complexity is, in large part, explained by the fact that it grew out of opposition to the widespread trust in the rational scientific modes of inquiry that dominated European and North American scholarship from the Enlightenment of the 1700s to the middle of the twentieth century. In the 1960s and 1970s, more and more theorists began to criticize the past 200 years of European-American theory for assuming that the world can be grasped fully by universal theories and rigorous research. In the wake of two devastating world wars, rapid developments in new technologies, major shifts in patterns of globalization, the emergent political struggles of oppressed groups, the totalitarianism of Stalinist communism, and the spread and vitality of capitalism (in spite of Marxism's long-standing prediction of its imminent collapse), growing numbers of so-called postmodernists attacked totalizing social theories such as Marxism, the benevolence of science, and universal human progress. They argued that these grand visions were nothing more than illusions of the modern world. To paraphrase the French postmodernist Jean-François Lyotard (1984), the failure of traditional social theories to explain and predict the whole of the human condition meant that it had become virtually impossible to take seriously any of the traditional universal frameworks for interpreting social life. In the absence of universally applicable social theories—what Lyotard called "metanarratives"—what we are left with is a countless number of "little narratives," or local understandings, that is, partial truths and relative realities.

In keeping with its fundamental opposition to any perspective claiming the power to lay bare the essence of the human condition, postmodern theory does not aim to develop a new system of thought through which the totality of social life can be understood. Rather, postmodernism aims to interrogate, disrupt, destabilize, deconstruct—to tear the stuffing from, really—any and all dominant theoretical approaches. One of the taken-for-granted ideas most often and most brutally battered by postmodern theorizing is the assumption that there is such a thing as an independently existing reality. To be sure, not every thinker who embraces postmodern ideals would be comfortable shouting "Reality does not exist!" from the rooftops—though no doubt some would. However, in light of the postmodern rejection of there being any fixed standard of meaning that exists independently from the endless play of symbolic representation, postmodern theory finds it very difficult to accept the existence of truth, certainty, objectivity, and reality.

According to the *OED Online* (2009), the word "reality" refers to "the aggregate of real things or existences; that which underlies and is the truth of appearances of phenomena." In other words, the traditional understanding of the concept, the one that guided the bulk of social theory prior to the middle of the twentieth century, is that reality is what *is*—regardless of the interpretations or representations of the people confronting it and regardless of whether it is *mis*interpreted or *mis*represented or, indeed, not interpreted or not represented in the first place. Even phenomenology, which, you will remember, called attention to the role of consciousness in shaping our access to reality, "examined not just what I happened to perceive when I looked at a particular rabbit, but the *universal essence* of rabbits and of the act of perceiving them" (Eagleton 1996, 49; emphasis added). The phenomenological viewpoint recognized that reality is grasped only in very complex ways, but, at root, phenomenology holds that reality does not depend upon anything other than itself to exist. Not so, says the postmodernist.

Postmodern theory denies that anything exists independently from the endless sets of symbolic relationships that tie together all things with all other things. In this view, meaning is produced not through presence but through *difference*. This word, or that flag, or these sounds, or those stones mean what they mean not because of any intrinsic connection between the word, flag, sounds, or stones and whatever it is that they are being used to represent. On the contrary, symbols derive their meaning through the position that they occupy within an infinitely complex and malleable

system of signs. For example, when appearing in close succession and in a particular order, the letters "b," "o," "o,"
"k," refer to the object that you're staring at right now,
but they do so not because of any deep-seated connection
between the word "book" itself and the material object that
English-speaking people call books. "Book" is able to refer
to what it does because, among English speakers, it doesn't
refer to the things labelled "cat" or "house" or "blind date"
or "old age" or "snorkelling" or "three-toed sloth" and so on
and so forth. The English language has different words and
symbols for those objects and activities—the ones listed in
the last sentence, for example—and although those symbols
also convey meaning within a particular cultural system, they
are no more natural expressions of their referents (the things
that they symbolize) than the word "book" is of the book in
your hand. Symbols are vessels of meaning; meaning does not
inhere within them.

It is not difficult to derive a certain bizarre pleasure from
pausing for a moment and reflecting upon the rather arbitrary
relationships between symbols and the things that they represent. Imagine thousands of people in a sports arena saluting
a flag with a donut emblazoned on the centre (or a skunk, or
a flat tire, or dog droppings) instead of a flag with a symbol
that we have grown to associate with moral fortitude. Why
not? The relationship between signifiers (the symbols used to
represent things) and signifieds (the things being represented)
is a product of specific historical and cultural contexts, not
of an eternal and universal standard of truth. Yet, important
as it is to grasp this way of thinking about language, meaning, and signification (the process through which a signifier
represents a signified), a fuller understanding of the threat that
postmodern thinking poses to reality requires an additional
step. After all, can't it just be that humans happen to give odd,
rather random names to the things around them, when, in
fact, reality just goes on existing whether we call what you're
reading a book or a cat or a three-toed sloth?

Making the presumption that reality (or "the aggregate of
real things or existences") simply goes on existing no matter

how humans happen to represent it is exactly what the post-modernist refuses to do. For, once it is established that the relationship between signifier and signified rests upon nothing more than the fact that each signifying relationship is different from every other, then the whole realm of representation "begins to look much more like a sprawling limitless web where there is a constant interchange and circulation of elements, where none of the elements is absolutely definable and where everything is caught up and traced through by everything else. [And] if this is so, then it strikes a serious blow at certain traditional theories of meaning" (Eagleton 1996, 112). It points to a world in which meaning—whether the meaning of a poem or television show or the meaning of "goodness" or of life itself—is never fixed in one place; rather, meaning is always on the move.

The fact that words, expressions, metaphors, and other symbols are only meaningful in relation to other words, expressions, and so on, means that they are all susceptible to break down, or at least to change shape, at the slightest probing or rereading. According to Derrida, statements and actions in all spheres of life are shot through with multiple meanings and can be "transformed when recontextualized, that is through being inserted into different narratives, compared with other texts, and so on" (Moran 2000, 435). Therefore, postmodernism threatens earlier conceptions of reality because it operates on the assumption that there can be nothing—no standard of truth, no universal moral code, no clear separation between image and illusion—that exists outside of the endless, arbitrary, and unstable relationship between signifiers and signifieds. As David McNally (2001, 58) explains, postmodern theory presumes that "there is nothing, no thing-in-itself, that can escape representation by signs. There is, in short, nothing we might access behind signs or outside of representation." There is no "aggregate of real things"; there is only representation—incomplete, flawed, skittish, unwieldy, deceitful representation.

One of the most influential and compelling examples of this sort of theorizing in practice is Judith Butler's work on the fiction of gender differences. Butler is a feminist cultural critic whose work has been greatly influenced by the writings of Jacques Derrida. She aims to break down traditional binary ways of thinking about gender identities by arguing that there is no such thing as a "man" or a "woman" apart from cultural practices and dominant forms of representation and interpretation. According to Butler (1988, 519), gender as a way of categorizing differences among human beings is not a natural or eternal distinction; it "is in no way a stable identity." On the contrary, says Butler, gender is a performance sustained "through a *stylized repetition of acts*" (italics in original). To say that gender is "performed" or "acted" is not to say that it is faked or that there is no such thing as gender. Gender is extremely powerful in its ability to organize social life, and, as was already noted in this chapter, "those who fail to do their gender right [to give a proper gender performance] are regularly punished"—mocked, excluded, beaten, or worse (Butler 1988, 522).

However, argues Butler, the right way "to do" gender—the ability to replicate socially sanctioned ways of being a man or a woman—is not the product of biology (or reality) but of learning how to act normally, how to represent the self properly, while growing up inside a particular cultural system. Butler (1988, 523) understands that, from a very early age, our bodies are forced to participate in an unending series of gender performances that (in most cases) make it seem as though each person *is in possession* of a specific gender identity; however, she maintains that gender identity does not exist within each person or in "reality" but that "the body becomes its gender through a series of acts which are renewed, revised, and consolidated through time." In sum, Butler does not believe that gender pre-exists language; in her view, there is "no prediscursive reality of nature" of which gender is a mere reflection (Turner 2007, 497).

Although Butler's work offers powerful ways to counter the Western world's history of sexism, the contribution of postmodern theory is not always so clear. For example, Baudrillard's (1983) concept of the "hyperreal," which he uses to argue that Disneyland is the real world whereas everything outside Disneyland is illusory, may provide the pieces for some splendid academic mind game, and surely is a contender for first prize for shock value, but what lesson or transformative vision does it offer people who just lost their jobs, or the chronically ill, or the subjects of ongoing sexism and racism? Are we to shake off our troubles and go fishing, knowing that Baudrillard says that none of this is real anyway? The challenge of claiming that reality doesn't exist is that reality keeps getting in the way. Developing bold assertions about the nonexistence of reality may be seen as a kind of conceptual triumph, but in working to show that there is no sturdy floor to social life, postmodernism ends up pulling the rug out from under anyone attempting to build a case about how the world works and how it could be changed for the better. In the words of Terry Eagleton (1996, 125), assuming a postmodern theoretical stance

> frees you at a stroke from having to assume a position on important issues, since what you say of such things will be no more than a passing product of the signifier and so in no sense to be taken as "true" or "serious." A further benefit of this stance is that it is mischievously radical in respect of everyone else's opinions, able to unmask the most solemn declarations as mere disheveled plays of signs, while utterly conservative in every other way. Since it commits you to affirming nothing, it is as injurious as blank ammunition.

Thinking Point: Competing Realities

The construction of reality in the world becomes particularly charged when we consider how it defines the horizons of possibility for our actions. The conflict and social order models provide contending visions of the workings of the world that frame our understanding of what it is realistic to expect in a particular situation. One model's hard-headed realism might seem like idealistic nonsense from the other's perspective. Gigantic tax cuts are the realistic solution to all of our problems from the point of view of some, while others think those cuts will only make things worse for much of the population.

The political debate over globalization over the last 20 years has been, in part, a debate about what is realistic. One side believes that jumping into the globalized world economy with both feet is the only realistic option because we are seeing an inevitable trend that we cannot challenge. The other argues that it is possible to resist these pressures because forces exist to make a better reality.

Globalization describes a set of changes in the operation of the world economy over the past 40 years, including shifts in the patterns of trade, production, investment, and international relations. There has been a great deal of debate about its costs and benefits. The social order and conflict models frame our understanding of contemporary globalization in very different ways and offer contending perspectives on whether it is realistic to accept its inevitable march or to mobilize against it. You should try to figure out which of the arguments below fits with the conflict model and which with the social order model, referring back to the discussion of the two perspectives in Chapter 2. Your goal here should be to clarify the basis upon which you link the argument to the appropriate model, finding as many details as possible that fit the core logic of the approach. Write an "S" beside statements you associate with the social order model and a "C" with statements you associate with conflict theory. Be prepared to explain to a friend why you've made these associations. What is it about them that links to core premises of one or the other theoretical perspective?

Argument A: A Better World Is Realistic

In this view, it is realistic to fight back against the forces of globalization, which is a political strategy that strengthens the position of the most powerful nations and corporations at the expense of the disadvantaged. The reality of globalization is an increasing gap between rich and poor within and between nations. It is a myth that globalization is about lowering barriers between nations and uniting us all in a new society that spans the globe and benefits us all.

The reality is that obstacles to the movement of people across borders have actually increased over the last 30 years, with the very specific exception of agreements such as the European Union, which allow increased mobility within a region for those who are already on the inside. The power of corporations to invest wherever they choose has been increased, but the ability of people to move has been limited by more restrictive immigration controls and refugee laws.

Globalization has stripped away some of the limited protection disadvantaged people had won from the ups and downs of the world economy, such as subsidies on key foodstuffs in Mexico, which made these foods affordable for the poorer sections of the population. Meanwhile, subsidies of hundreds of millions of dollars flow to corporations to lure auto plants to particular jurisdictions.

The shift in power towards corporations is also reinforced in trade agreements such as the North American Free Trade Agreement (NAFTA). These agreements include provisions that allow companies to sue governments to overturn democratic decisions that might hamper a corporation's ability to make profits. The decisions on these suits are made by secret tribunals. The prime imperative driving globalization is to reduce impediments to profit making in whatever form they might appear.

The forces that favour globalization are powerful indeed, yet that does not mean the process cannot be contested. In France, Argentina, and Bolivia, people have fought back and forced governments to overturn new policies aligned with the process of globalization. Demonstrations have greeted almost every multilateral meeting aimed at promoting the globalization agenda. The powerful have found a new strategy in globalization, one that strengthens their position, but the disadvantaged have the potential, over time, to develop new forms of resistance to assert their own power. That potential is the basis for a realistic sense that a better world is possible.

Argument B: Get Real: Globalization Is Inevitable

Resistance to globalization is as futile as mobilizing for round-the-clock sunshine to keep the streets safer. There is a new reality out there, and our choice is to join in or get left behind. Globalization provides an opportunity to export the benefits of modern industrial society around the world. The best way to help the people of the poorer nations is to allow them a competitive place in the world market. Previously, trade barriers served to insulate the economies of the most developed countries from competition.

At the same time, Soviet-style economic measures focused on state control limited the economic development of many of the less-developed nations.

Globalization combines the opening up of the economies of the less-developed nations with new trade agreements that increase the global circulation of goods and investment. Over time, these twin processes will provide people in the poorer nations the opportunity to advance. There might be some short-term dislocation effects, but these temporary setbacks will be overcome as modern economies develop and thrive around the world.

The move towards globalization results from tremendous technological advances, including the computer, the spread of air travel, and breakthroughs in telecommunications. As a result, information, goods, and people can travel the globe more quickly than ever before. These technological innovations have corresponded to political changes associated with the fall of the Soviet Union and the shift of China towards more open economic development.

There are always those who oppose progress and try to keep things the way they used to be. Globalization offers unprecedented opportunities for trade and development. It must be given a chance to work. Investment and trade are the basis for a future of economic growth that will raise the conditions of the life of humanity around the planet. Those who choose not to participate will be left behind in economic and political backwaters. It may not be pretty, but that is reality.

Before moving on, design and conduct a systematic way of analysing arguments A and B with the aim of identifying which reflects a social order perspective and which reflects a conflict perspective.

6

Nature and Culture: The Social Construction of Distinctions

Nature is one of the key concepts framing the perspectives of many social theories. Most theories have a central vision of **human nature** and assumptions about our relationship with the environment we find ourselves living in. This chapter begins with a discussion of the relationship between nature and culture in our understanding of the human experience.

The way we see the relationship between nature and culture underpins our vision of human nature, the core characteristics of people across time and through space. Every theoretical school is based on a set of assumptions about the core constituents of human nature.

The whole question of what is natural in human behaviour is hotly debated. After all, the things that are natural might be thought to be impossible to change through deliberate human activity. In Chapter 2, we saw how government officials depict economic crises as natural (and therefore unavoidable) parts of life when comparing a severe recession to a once-in-a-lifetime tsunami. The idea that the economic boom-and-bust cycle is as natural as the cycle of the seasons is reinforced when economists talk about looking for "green shoots" (for example, rising stock prices and other positive economic indicators) to signal that prosperity is just around the corner. Certainly, there *are* facts of nature. Death, for example, is a prime fact of life, and no amount of human activity will ever overcome it. The point that we need to be concerned about is that theories often naturalize—that is, they treat products of human activity as if they were products of immutable forces. It is worth asking to what extent this kind of naturalizing is reflected in the language of tsunamis, green shoots, rotten assets, and so on in the capitalist economy. The whole discussion of nature in the early twenty-first century necessarily raises the questions of ecology and the health of our environment. Theory can cast climate change as something we can work on or as an inevitable fact of life.

THE REASONS WE COOK

IF YOU think back on everything you ate over the last 24 hours, there is a good chance that much of it was cooked. We cook or process so much of our food that it seems obvious to do so. People claim that food tastes better or is healthier when cooked. Yet many foods lose valuable nutrients through the cooking process, and the preference for raw or cooked food is highly subjective. Fish can be eaten raw (sushi), steak can be eaten raw (steak tartare), and we all know that carrots can be eaten raw. Yet we persist in cooking many foods that can be eaten raw.

The anthropologist Claude Lévi-Strauss (1969) argues that cooking is primarily a symbolic process through which we translate foodstuffs from the realm of nature (raw) to the realm of culture (cooked). Cooking food is, after all, a uniquely human characteristic. In the world of nature, there is no other species that processes what it eats in a similar way. Lévi-Strauss suggests that this symbolic dimension to cooking is far more important than any ideas about taste or health. Indeed, he would argue that our taste for food prepared in particular ways or our ideas about what is healthy follow upon this symbolic process of making food into culture.

So cooking is a process by which we transform the things we are about to eat from nature to culture. Cooking, therefore, establishes a symbolic relationship between the cultural and the natural. Indeed, Lévi-Strauss says that all human cultures seek to locate themselves relative to nature in many of their most common practices. He is a structuralist theorist who argues that the most important dimensions of social practices are often not visible to those who participate in them. Underlying the stated goals of many social practices is the deep symbolic code reproducing the notion that culture is superior to nature.

People might explain their surface reasons for cooking food, cutting hair, or wearing clothes, but underlying their explanations is a shared commitment to practices that stake claims for the superiority of the cultural over the natural.

Sherry Ortner (1974) points out that this relationship of culture and nature has distinct implications for our understanding of gender. The symbolic systems that rank culture above nature also rank men above women, as it is assumed that women are closer to nature due to their association with childbirth and breastfeeding. One of the sources of sexist and patriarchal assumptions is, therefore, this practice of valuing the cultural above the natural.

At a time when we are becoming ever more aware of the ecological costs of certain human practices, it is certainly important to investigate whether some of our core cultural assumptions put us on a collision course with the earth by devaluing the natural. There are, of course, great debates about the theories of Lévi-Strauss and about the idea that deep cultural meanings operate beneath the awareness of human actors. It is worth reflecting on the presumption of anthropologists of European ancestry, who thought that they understood the true meanings of the cultural actions of Indigenous peoples better than the participants themselves.

The relationship of the natural and the cultural is one of the central themes in humanities and social science theories. One of the ongoing debates about the relationship between nature and the human condition is the nature versus nurture discussion about the relative influence of genetic heritage and cultural upbringing on the development of the individual. The fundamental premises of all social theories include certain assumptions about the relationship between humanity and nature. The idea of "human nature" is also regularly debated in the political sphere, where policies ranging from welfare cuts to tougher criminal sentences are justified in terms of the fundamental motivational structure presumed to underlie all human actions.

It is not our aim in this chapter to resolve these debates about nature and culture definitively. Rather, we want to show the way that theoretical reflection disturbs our easy assumptions about this relationship. For example, it is important to think about whether or not there is any meaningful boundary between nature and culture or whether all cultural activity is "natural."

GOING AGAINST NATURE

THE IDEA that certain practices are unnatural for humans is frequently expressed in ethical debates about norms and regulations. For example, people opposed to homosexuality often describe same-sex sexual practices as "unnatural." The extent to which human sexual practices are natural or cultural plays a large part in debates about the regulation of sexuality. For instance, some argue that sexual restraint is cultural, distinguishing us from other species that respond to the urges of heat by indiscriminate sexual activity. Others argue that heterosexuality is natural, though it is pretty hard to argue that any particular sexual mode predominates throughout the natural world.

Our thinking about nature and culture often operates on the assumption that these are separate and opposed. Specifically, culture tends to be conceived of as the things created or shaped by humans, and nature is presumed to be everything else—the stuff that existed prior to and independently of human contact. Human culture, however, can be understood as a product of evolution governed by natural laws, which produced a species with the capacity, indeed the need, for culture. There is nothing "unnatural" about culture, as it is itself a part of nature. It does not really make sense, then, to label certain human practices as "unnatural." The idea that what is cultural is by definition also natural is an important challenge to the standard assumptions we make about nature and culture.

Terry Eagleton, in his study of the history of English words, points out that the term "culture" derived from ideas of nature. The term originally described human work on nature to shape spontaneous growth: "We derive our word for the finest of human activities from labour and agriculture, crops and cultivation" (Eagleton 2000, 1). The idea of culture originated as a description for the activity of cultivation, the process of intervening in natural growth processes to have an impact on the outcome, such as more wheat and fewer "weeds." There are, of course, no "weeds" in nature— that is a completely human-oriented term to describe the natural growth we determine to be inconvenient.

The term culture, then, presumes a relationship with nature from the outset, according to Eagleton (2000, 3): "Nature produces culture which changes nature." There is, then, nothing strictly "unnatural" about the development of a city, which is merely a particular act of cultivation in which raw materials are brought together in specific ways to make streets and buildings (see Eagleton 2000, 4). Even the most artificial synthetics grow out of human work on the natural world (extracting, recombining, synthesizing).

The term "culture" is therefore very rich, as it refers to the complex interchange between conscious human actors and their natural environment. "Human beings are not mere products of their environs, but neither are these environs sheer clay for their self-fashioning. If culture transfigures nature, it is a project to which nature sets rigorous limits" (Eagleton 2000, 5). Humans do not, for example, override the laws of gravity when they fly in airplanes but work within them to produce levitation. In this sense, human action involves important components of agency (work on the environment to meet one's own goals) and determinism (the overriding impact of the environment due to the unalterable character of certain structural conditions).

HUMAN NATURE

THE RELATIONSHIP between culture and nature is particularly important in debates about human nature. These debates raise the issues of the essence of the human condition and the extent to which this is biologically given or socially constructed. You may have heard someone in class or on the news ask whether it was "nature or nurture" that led a person to behave a certain way. Why did this man turn out to be a police officer and that one start to rob banks? Are their brains wired differently, or was there something about their life experiences that put each on a different path? The nature versus nurture question is an important iteration of the whole debate over what is nature and what is culture. We all tend to make assumptions about human nature all the time in our interactions, which are based on our attributing to others varying degrees of trust, love, generosity, suspicion, hatred, or greed.

One view of human nature that is very influential in contemporary North American debates is reflected in the novel *Lord of the Flies*, which we discussed briefly in Chapter 2. In this view, society is the thin civilizing line that protects people from their own worst selves, which are fearful, greedy, impulsive, and susceptible to melting into a violent mindless mass. Conservative political movements and politicians frequently invoke this view of humanity to justify law-and-order regimes and military conquests.

Lord of the Flies traces the experiences of a group of children who find themselves alone on a deserted island. At first, it's a dreamworld without adult authority. Early on, a boy named Ralph says with a smile, "No grown-ups" (Golding 1958, 8). But in the absence of that adult authority, things go rotten pretty quickly. The boys miss being rescued because the signal fire goes out when the fire tenders leave their posts to go hunting (Golding 1958, 75). Most of the boys join a murderous mass and kill a boy as they chant, "Kill the beast! Cut his throat! Spill his blood!" (Golding 1958, 168).

The naval officer who finally rescues them is a bit shocked at the condition of these British boys: "I should have thought that a pack of British boys—you're all British aren't you?—would have been able to put up a better show than that. . . ." Ralph replies, "It was like that at first . . . before things—" (Golding 1958, 222). This image of Britishness as the thin civilizing line flows through the book, revealing the racist assumptions underlying this view of human nature, which divides people into civilized and savage. At one point, Piggy asks, "Which is better—to be a pack of painted niggers like you are or to be sensible like Ralph is?" (Golding 1958, 199).

According to this concept of human nature, then, children must be civilized by years of socialization to learn to restrain the "savage" within and live by the rules. Children are dangerous because they have not yet been domesticated. Adult supervision is crucial at all times to protect children from their own impulses.

A very different view of human nature is presented in Marge Piercy's novel *Woman on the Edge of Time* (1979). This book explores a utopian society envisioned by a woman who is actually locked in an asylum. Here, the children are given as much freedom as possible in a nurturing atmosphere to explore the world and create themselves as persons. They do not go to school but mix freely with adults and play at many activities to learn by engaging with their environment. In this way, children and adults are constantly learning:

> But who wants to grow up with a head full of facts in boxes? We never leave school and go to work. We're always working and always studying. We think, what a person thinks [she or he] knows has to be tried out all the time, placed against what people need. We care a lot about *how* things are done. (Piercy 1979, 131)

A visitor from the present wonders how someone can do repair work with a "mob of kids underfoot." The guide from this utopia replies, "A mob of kids? . . . We think about kids so differently it makes us crosstalk, my friend. . . . We ask a lot of our children but . . . politely" (Piercy 1979, 132).

In this view of human nature, society is seen as enabling, but also potentially restricting, the creativity of the child and of the person. When the visitor from our time hears that children set out on their own at age 12 to pursue a vision quest in the woods she is outraged. Her guide replies,

> We haven't misplaced a child yet. You're right, accidents happen. . . . But why try to control everything? . . . [W]e think control interferes with pleasure and with communing and we care about both. (Piercy 1979, 117)

In *Lord of the Flies*, human nature threatens to slip out of control if it is not properly regulated by society. In contrast, in *Woman on the Edge of Time*, social control threatens to stifle the creativity that is the essence of human nature. These fundamentally opposed visions of human nature are connected to very different views of education, politics, and social theory.

There are, then, strongly opposed visions of human nature that underlie our everyday understanding of nature and culture. It is worth spending some time trying to understand your own vision of human nature; it likely has a significant impact on your political assumptions and your interpersonal behaviour. One of the most important features of effective theoretical thinking is that it makes us more aware of our own key assumptions when looking at the world, and it helps us understand those of others.

Thinking Point: Debates about Human Nature

It is often easy to stir up a fairly intense debate about approaches to crime and law enforcement. Some people believe very strongly in capital punishment, tough sentences, and firm police actions. Others oppose capital punishment, support rehabilitation, and are suspicious of police power. These positions are often based on fundamental assumptions about human nature.

Those who favour capital punishment, stricter sentences, and more policing tend to be fairly pessimistic about the possibility of reforming lawbreakers, assuming that patterns of criminality are quite firmly set and difficult to change. This view of criminality often builds on the idea that socialization is the only thing that tames humans, who otherwise would be quite savage and beastly.

The criminal is the beast who comes to the surface due to a failure of socialization, either because the agents of society (e.g., parents, schools, and community) failed or because the individual has a particularly savage nature. In any case, by the time the behaviour has reached the point of criminality, little can be done but to restrain the beast.

In contrast, those who are suspicious of law enforcement tend to be more optimistic about rehabilitation, assuming that the human being is fairly plastic, susceptible to being moulded and remoulded by effective agencies of society. This perspective is founded on the premise that humans are creative social beings who become dangerous only when they have been brutalized by individuals or social institutions. One of the dangers of an oppressive society, according to this perspective, is that it breeds brutalization, for example, in prison. The aim, therefore, is to intervene in processes of socialization to reshape the person in a more positive, prosocial (as opposed to antisocial) direction.

In these debates about law enforcement, people often talk past one another because their fundamental assumptions are so different that there is little common ground for discussion. These conflicting perspectives on human nature often resurface in debates about education, poverty, housing, and the family. The question of whether the goal is to overcome the beast within or to unleash potential creative powers underlies many of our discussions. At this moment, which side in these debates do you feel is more persuasive? Make a point-form list of what evidence and assumptions have gone into shaping your current feelings. Now imagine that you are arguing in favour of the opposing point of view. What would be the best line of criticism to challenge your original position?

NATURALIZATION

THE CONCEPT of human nature is a powerful reference point in many debates about politics and society. One of the most important ways that this concept enters into these debates is through the process of **naturalization**, which treats the products of human action as if they were the inevitable outcome of natural laws beyond human control. In other words, we tend to naturalize social conditions associated with a particular kind of social structure at a particular moment in time. We consider them as a natural product. Naturalization therefore places some things outside the realm of political debate, suggesting that they are simple facts of life that we must ultimately accept. How dare we argue for lesbian, gay, or transgender relations when heterosexuality is supposedly "natural"?

One of the major features of racism, for example, is that it naturalizes differences that are a product of particular social and cultural circumstances. Stuart Hall (1999a, 445) writes that racism "operates by constructing impassable symbolic boundaries between racially-constituted categories . . . and attempts to fix and naturalize the difference between belonging and otherness." A particular colour of skin or type of hair is taken as the symbolic marker of who really belongs here and who is an outsider (even after generations). It's not that there's no such thing as different coloured skin—of course there is. The point is that racism attributes specific qualities and values on the basis of, for example, skin colour. People have different lengths of tongues, different laughs, different patterns in their palm lines, different numbers of hairs on their legs—there are countless ways to divide up the human species. The fact is, however, that racism invests specific physical differences (such as skin colour) with deep meaning and ignores others (such as different tongue lengths, and so on). Following Hall, we could argue that racism in Canada is premised on these ideas of belonging and otherness in that some people are seen as more naturally "Canadian" than others. And this distinction is not based simply on seniority, as Aboriginal people have been excluded from Canadianness historically through both the destruction of their own cultures and their marginalized status. It is based on a particular series of historical events and conquests that developed a particular power structure associated with specific ideas of whiteness.

Naturalization treats human categories as fixed features of the natural world, as characteristics not subject to change.

This view can create a sense of resignation, an acceptance of conditions as they are. If it is going to rain tomorrow, there is little you can do but carry an umbrella. It is absolutely futile to rage at the weather, organize a protest movement, or vote for those candidates who promise warmth and sunshine in the middle of a northern winter. However, if a factory is being closed, or a dangerous chemical is discharged into the air or water, or a person is being deported or evicted, someone somewhere is making a decision. As long as there are human beings making decisions, it is always at least hypothetically possible that others can have some impact on that decision. The weather, by contrast, is not produced directly by human decisions, though it is possible that the long-term impact of human actions is changing the world's weather map. In that case, global warming is a product of human decisions and therefore susceptible to social action, but tomorrow's weather is not a result of our activities and therefore cannot be changed by us.

Naturalization can occur in times when there is not a lot of protest action around, when it may feel futile to try to change things, rather like demonstrating against a rainy day. In these circumstances, naturalization takes place because people resign themselves to the way things are. Nigel Harris (1971, 57) writes that this comes from the perception of powerlessness, "which usually underpins what is called 'apathy,' the knowledge that no action by oneself can change matters." The condition that upsets us begins to appear to be part of the natural order, just like the weather, in that there seems to be nothing that can be done about it.

Naturalization can therefore be an important component of ideologies. "Ideology" is a highly contentious term in social theory (Bailey and Gayle 2003). Here, we will define ideologies as the explanatory frameworks used by particular social groups (such as ethnic groups and social classes) to guide their action in the world (Hall 1999b, 26). Ideologies base a system of thought on an interpretation of the way the world looks from a particular social position. As we discussed in Chapter 4, for example, the classroom might look different from the position of a teacher or a student. Similarly, you look at a fast-food restaurant in a very different way if you are there as a customer, a worker, or a visiting executive from head office.

Ideologies systematize and package the insights that can be obtained from a particular perspective, for example, that of labour or management. A pro-management ideology might base its world view on the claim that everyone gains advantages through economic growth resulting from rising productivity and cost savings to gain international competitiveness. In contrast, a pro-labour ideology might focus on the costs workers bear for increased productivity, for example, in the form of layoffs, increased injury rates, or greater stress. The process of systematizing and packaging these ideologies involves important elements of interpretation, as certain features are highlighted and others ignored.

Naturalization is a common feature of such ideological perspectives. A pro-management ideology might treat the competitive environment rather like the weather (there is nothing we can do about it) and therefore frame our reality in such a way that we see productivity increases and cost savings as inevitable. A factory might have to be closed or the pensions of retired people dramatically cut, but that is simply the cost of doing business, and there is no other way. For example, during the civic workers strike in Toronto in 2009, pro-management voices argued that the union would have to accept concessions because of the economic crisis. It didn't matter that workers didn't cause the crisis and that different municipal workers were offered better contracts only months earlier. The only thing that pro-business voices cared about was resuming public services at a cheaper-than-ever cost. At the same time, the advocates who fight to save jobs and pensions might be criticized from a pro-management perspective for naturalizing entitlements, assuming workers have a right to a job and a pension regardless of their own productivity or the overall health of the economy.

Ideologies often seem completely false from the perspective of those who oppose them and absolutely true to their advocates. The reality is often more complex—ideologies that have the power to grip people tend to have some sort of real basis even if that is combined with elements of distortion based on partiality. There are two important distortions that often distinguish ideologies: eternalization and naturalization (Hall 1999b, 33). Naturalization, as we have already discussed, consists of treating the outcome of human actions as if they were products of nature rather than of particular historical processes. Eternalization is the claim that a condition arising in a particular circumstance at a particular moment is true for all time. For example, some people claim that it is natural for humans to be greedy and selfish, basing that argument on observations of the ways we behave in an industrial capitalist society that prizes acquisitiveness highly. Greed has not necessarily played the same role in some of the other cultures anthropologists study, cultures in which orientation towards the group as opposed to the individual is the crucial basis of human interaction. David McNally (2006, 271) has shown that, over the past two centuries, representative government has come to be seen as the natural way of organizing democracy, whereas, in fact, in ancient Greece, rule of the people "meant the sovereignty of citizens over all aspects of social and political life." Democracy began as something much more "active, meaningful and participatory than what goes by the name of representative democracy today" (McNally 2006, 270).

Thinking Point: The Ideology of Laziness

"Students are lazy." It is quite common to hear this complaint from professors. Many university teachers feel that students who miss classes, read as little as possible of the course material, and do minimal work on their assignments are lazy. Yet these same students might be highly motivated in the gym, at their job, or in a club. Their laziness may, in short, be situational rather than general. Situational laziness may result from many circumstances: a lack of interest in the subject matter, a feeling that actually being in class doesn't matter because very little seems to happen there, or a sense that passing is sufficient to get the degree and that is what is important.

The claim that students are lazy is rooted in a larger ideological premise: the idea that people are fundamentally disinclined to work. This premise seems to be confirmed every time someone is seen leaning on a shovel rather than digging with it, cheating on an assignment by downloading it rather than doing the work, or chatting with a friend on the phone when a customer is wanting service. It seems that people need to be motivated by money or grades or fear or some other external factor.

The ideological premise that people are lazy often includes elements of naturalization and eternalization. Laziness is naturalized when it is seen as a fundamental characteristic of the species, a part of human nature. In this view, the inbuilt goal of humans is to minimize effort. The eternalization of laziness occurs when we assume that a pattern of action in a particular moment is the product of an impulse that is there for all time. Thus, students who do only the bare minimum of work in a university course are taken as indicators that the flight from work is a permanent feature of the human condition.

The discussion of abstraction in Chapter 4 examined how particular concepts get framed, focusing on the dimensions of extension (coverage of time and place), level of generality, and vantage point. Ideologies frame concepts like laziness in particular ways. Theoretical thinking involves the ability to understand the ways key concepts are framed in particular discussions. Among the people you know, think of someone you might characterize as lazy. Imagine now another explanation for the pattern of behaviour you have labelled as laziness.

ECOLOGY

IN HER novel *O Pioneers!*, originally published in 1913, Willa Cather portrays the experiences of white settlers on the plains of Nebraska. Early in the novel, she records the dismay of a young boy whose family has just arrived:

> But the great fact was the land itself, which seemed to overwhelm the little beginnings of human society that

> struggled in its somber wastes. It was from facing this
> vast hardness that the boy's mouth had become so bitter;
> because he felt that men were too weak to make any mark
> here, that the land wanted to be alone, to preserve its
> own fierce strength, its peculiar, savage kind of beauty, its
> uninterrupted mournfulness. (Cather 1993, 5–6)

Of course, the aloneness of the land was largely an artefact of the white viewpoint that refused to see Aboriginal peoples and their prior relationship with it. Nonetheless, this portrait is a reminder that the land can seem greater than humanity and nature a more potent force than culture.

At the beginning of the twenty-first century, we may find it hard to credit the land with this power. Certainly, there are moments when the grandeur of the land and the force of nature seem awesome. But, in the age of the atomic bomb, environmental devastation, and greenhouse-induced global warming, Mother Earth is looking a bit vulnerable these days. Over the course of the twentieth century, something happened in human relations with the planet and in the social consciousness of that relationship. The combination of social and technological change has produced a situation in which we have a unique responsibility for the health of the planet, whether we wish to assume it or not. Rachel Carson's pioneering book *Silent Spring* (1962) was a pathfinder in the development of a new awareness of the hazards people were creating, and it spawned activism against pollution and the degradation of the environment.

Humanity has a huge responsibility for the ecology of the planet at the beginning of this century. David Harvey clarifies:

> A strong case can be made that the humanly induced
> environmental transformations now under way are larger
> scale, riskier, and more far-reaching and complex in their
> implications (materially, spiritually, aesthetically) than
> ever before in human history. . . . The quantitative shifts
> that have occurred in the last half of the twentieth century
> in, for example, scientific knowledge and engineering

> capacities, industrial output, waste generation, invention
> of new chemical compounds, urbanization, population
> growth, international trade, fossil fuel consumption,
> resource extraction, habitat modification—just to name
> some of the most important features—imply a qualitative
> shift in environmental impacts and potential unintended
> consequences that require a comparable qualitative shift in
> our responses and our thinking. (Harvey 2000, 120)

That is quite a list, and he did not even discuss nuclear, chemical, or biological weapons.

It is, however, misleading to discuss the responsibility of humanity (as we did above) in ways that make it sound as if all people bear this weight equally. Eduardo Galeano (2001, 216) makes this case strongly: "The state of the world's health is disgusting, and official rhetoric extrapolates in order to absolve: 'We are all responsible' is the lie technocrats offer and politicians repeat, meaning no one is responsible." The consumption of the wealthier nations of the earth is massively out of proportion with that of the rest of humanity, creating a huge environmental toll. Galeano (2001, 223) illustrates this disproportionate responsibility and benefit with the example of the flower industry: "Colombia grows tulips for Holland and roses for Germany. . . . When the flowers are ready, Holland gets the tulips, Germany gets the roses, and Colombia gets lower wages, damaged land, and poisoned water."

As Harvey (2000, 221) writes, "environmental impacts frequently have a social bias (class, racial, and gender discriminations are evident in, say, the location of toxic waste sites and the global impacts of resource depletion or environmental degradation)." If you map exposures to dangerous substances, toxic dump sites, and hazardous processes, you find patterns that show, for example, that working-class people, people of colour, and people in the countries of the developing world face the gravest dangers and get the fewest benefits. Lisa Parks (2004, 50) has written about whole villages in China that are literally built upon electronic waste from the First World: "Here wire from the West's obsolete computers becomes the earth's ground floor, and . . . as machines are disassembled, it is impossible to separate the village topography from the computer's insides." What people in the West often conceive of as the invisible world of "cyberspace" is clearly visible in the blotches on children's bodies caused by playing atop discarded keyboards, monitors, and ink cartridges.

Cancer frequently results from environmental exposures. Those on the front line for these exposures are disproportionately working-class people, people of colour, and people living in poverty. Matthew Firth, James Brophy, and Margaret Keith (1997, 2) claim that "Cancer is clearly a disease that affects workers and the economically disadvantaged more than other sectors of society." The impact of environmental degradation follows the contours of existing structures of social inequality. Those theorists who argue that the concept of social class is hopelessly outmoded in contemporary North American societies would do well to investigate the relative exposure levels of those who own and control the workplace and those who work in it.

The relationship between culture and nature is a charged one at the beginning of this century. Humans have, through our culture, developed the productive capacity to transform the face of the planet. Humans alone can turn huge valleys into lakes to make hydroelectric power, or they can produce sufficient quantities of greenhouse gases to threaten the integrity of the earth's environment. It is a uniquely human situation to bear responsibility for the survival or extinction of whole species, including, potentially, our own.

Being in this position does not mean that humans are above nature; we are still a part of it and subject to its laws. Yet we are a unique part as a result of the capacities we have developed through our culture to make our mark. Consequently, we have a tremendous responsibility to reflect and act on the relationship between nature and culture. Theoretical thinking can help prepare us for this work.

Andrew Biro (2005) provides an important example of the role of theoretical thinking in the development of an effective environmental politics. Biro calls for a kind of theorizing that is hard work; he proposes that we negotiate through opposed approaches to the relationship between humans and nature and draw on the constructive elements of each approach. On the one hand, he argues that we have much to learn from the postmodern critique of "nature" that focuses on the ways human conceptualizations of the natural are social constructions reflecting specific cultural assumptions. If you think back to the earlier discussion of postmodernism, you will not be surprised that the emphasis here is on the critique of key concepts and approaches. Postmodernists want us to understand the ways people summon up "nature" as a basis for authority in arguments, the ways we explain things in terms of impersonal and inalterable forces.

Biro grants that there is power in this critique of "nature," yet he argues that it is not by itself the basis for an effective ecological politics. Also important is trying to learn something from the perspective he describes as "ecocentric"—one that inverts the lens of many approaches to nature by attempting to start with the natural rather than with human activity. Ecocentric approaches are very critical of viewpoints that start with the needs and rights of humans while treating nature (living or inorganic) simply as objects of our actions.

In the end, Biro rejects both postmodern and ecocentric approaches but concludes that each has elements to offer in the development of a fuller analysis. He argues that ecological activists and thinkers need to reconcile "a defense of nature and a thoroughgoing critique of 'nature'" (Biro 2005, 3). Even if the idea of a "pollutant" is a social construct, the destruction of the ecosystem through the dumping of what humans define as "waste" has a devastating impact.

NOTHING MORE NATURAL
THAN CULTURE

THERE IS nothing new in the view that separates nature from culture. Stephen J. Gould points to the human habit of seeking to distinguish ourselves from nature, which he describes as "dichotomization, or division into two opposite categories, usually with attributions of value expressed as good or bad, or higher and lower." As a result of that division, we have sought for "a 'golden barrier,' a firm criterion to mark an unbridgeable gap between the mentality and behaviour of humans and all other creatures" (Gould 2002, 230).

Theoretical thinking helps us unpack the dichotomies that shape our perspective on many issues. A wide range of theoretical analyses on the relationship of nature to culture argue not only that culture is distinct from nature but that all of human life ought to be understood through the lens of culture—and that includes what is popularly thought to be nature, for even it only exists as "nature" through symbols, language, and patterns of human thought and representation. More moderately, it is also possible to argue that culture is a part of nature that bestows on people unique capacities to transform the environment.

Good theoretical thinking denaturalizes—it melts the lines of distinction that we take for granted in our everyday reflections on the world and raises debates about where such lines might be drawn. This process may seem tedious and unnecessary, a detailed investigation of things we already know. The challenge in theoretical thinking is to examine things we *think* we already know with open eyes, so that we are prepared to be surprised. This thinking does not mean giving up the perspectives and experiences that make us who we are; rather, it encourages us to take up a new kind of self-reflection so that we become more aware of the assumptions that frame our own vision of the world.

One of the most influential methods for theoretical reflection on social reality is to use models derived from the observation of the natural world. Indeed, as discussed in Chapter 1, there has been an ongoing circulation of models back and forth between the natural sciences, on the one hand, and the humanities and social sciences on the other. Darwin's conception of nature, which had a huge influence on social theory, was itself influenced by the political economy theories of Thomas Malthus.

A prominent example of the use of models derived from the natural world to explain the operation of human society is the organic analogy used by social order theorists. A long line of social theorists have argued that the workings of society are analogous to those of an organism. An analogy draws a parallel between two phenomena, reasoning that what happens in one case will also happen in the other when crucial elements are similar. The organic analogy has provided important tools for understanding interdependence, equilibrium, and evolutionary change in modern industrial societies—tools of analysis based on models drawn from nature.

This organic analogy began as a simple model of interdependence. Just as the human body can survive only if its differentiated organs (brain, lungs, heart) work together, so society, as a whole, is dependent for its survival on the series of specialized institutions (religion, government, schools) that it has developed. The development of the science of evolution through the 1800s inspired richer and more detailed versions of this organic analogy.

Theories of evolution, particularly those of Darwin, provided new materials for understanding the relationship between equilibrium and change as well as new ways of understanding differentiation and integration. The Darwinian account of evolution provided tools for seeing changes as incremental steps towards constructive adaptation to the environment. Random variations in the reproduction of species produce mutations that occasionally yield individual organisms more likely than others to survive and reproduce. The new mutations, such as a slightly longer beak that makes it easier to get insects out of bark or a slight variation in colouring that provides better camouflage, then become more numerous as the individuals with those characteristics have the best chance of surviving and producing a new generation.

These random variations are not produced out of any desire for change on the part of the species involved but are simply reproductive accidents. Indeed, in most cases, these mutations create individuals ill-suited for survival. Once in a while, though, the accident works for the better.

Over time, these accidents produce a natural world that is more highly differentiated and more integrated. The earliest life forms were simple one-celled organisms that were quite independent in that they could survive and reproduce on their own, without sex or any other interaction. As life forms became more complex, the cells within became more specialized and different from one another, as well as more interdependent. A brain cell, for example, could not survive on its own if it were cast onto the pavement in an accident.

At another level, ecosystems developed more complexity. More species evolved, becoming more specialized and more interdependent, each occupying a very specific niche in the chain of life.

More complex ecosystems are thus no less stable than the simpler ones. Change can produce a new kind of stability rooted in equilibrium on the basis of differentiation and integration. Thus, the idea of a society grounded in order draws on specific conceptions of stability in the natural realm.

Thinking Point: Your Research Matters

If you follow ecological debates at all, it will be clear that the well-being of future generations is at stake. Humans are making a huge impact on the environment, through the extinction of species, climate change, and the destruction of habitats. What you think and do about ecological issues will help shape your future.

Our current environmental situation means that the quality of your knowledge is important. You need to be able to assess the empirical basis and the analytical strength of your own views on ecological issues if you want to make a difference. That means your own research matters.

One of the great skills you can learn is how to use research to identify, investigate, and pose solutions to problems. Good theoretical thinking is a crucial part of your research tool chest. The following four questions will help you develop your skills for the important tasks of researching ecological issues and using theory effectively to deepen your analysis.

1. Identify an environmental issue that is currently being debated where you are. Find some statements that stake out opposed positions in these debates. How much are these debates about the facts, and how much are they about using different perspectives to interpret empirical data? How might you contribute to improving the quality of this debate?

2. Find an example of naturalization in current political debates. Identify a quotation and explain how it naturalizes. What would it mean to denaturalize what's being said in this quotation?

3. Consider the way the discussion of nature and culture in this chapter might be reframed through the perspective of Indigenous ways of knowing. Refer to the discussion of Indigenous ways of knowing in Chapter 1 to remind yourself of the key features of this perspective.

4. Find a picture of a suburban house and contrast it with a picture of a high-density apartment block. Examine the images and answer this question: "Who is living greener, the person living in this house or in the apartment building?" Explain your answer.

7

*Making Time: Clocking
Social Relations*

T HIS CHAPTER begins with time, which seems to be the most
natural of measures. After all, time passes in nature, lives
begin and end, seasons change, the sun rises and sets. This
chapter will show the ways that this apparently natural system
is deeply rooted in our social relations.

Clock time developed historically in the context of a specific set of changes to the way society worked. For centuries,
the Western world has been organized around clock time,
which has required the development of a technical apparatus ranging from accurate timepieces to a system of time
zones.

The increased focus on clock time might be understood in
terms of technological progress. In this chapter, however, we
argue that it is connected to particular power relations in society. Control over time has become a crucial means by which
the powerful exercise their control over society. This whole
issue seems particularly pressing given the great **speed-up** that
seems to be intensifying our time use at the present moment.
We are busy people and getting more so.

Theory helps us understand the issue of time by setting it
in the context of history, the patterns of change over time.
The clock that seems so central to our lives now was not so
important even a couple of generations ago. Historical understanding helps us distinguish the eternal features of the human
condition from those that change as society does.

The chapter concludes with sample arguments from the
social order and conflict models that contrast the approaches
to history associated with each. History is not simply an
account of what happened back in the day but also an interpretation of events framed by our assumptions about the

workings of the world. Different models therefore yield contrasting pictures of the same events.

As teachers, we often notice students watching the clock in our classrooms. It is usually a bit disheartening, as we do our best to keep things hopping. At the same time, we must confess that we have done our share of clock-watching in similar circumstances. One of the features of clock-watching is that time seems to go very slowly. You look again, and it seems the clock's hands have not moved at all.

In fact, the pace of time seems to vary a great deal in our daily lives. People telling the story of a car accident or a similar catastrophe will often say that time suddenly slowed down, the world went into slow motion. Meanwhile, a much-savoured weekend can fly right by so that, before you know it, you face yet another Monday morning. Julia Glass (2003, 194) expresses this idea beautifully in her novel *Three Junes*:

> Time plays like an accordion in the way it can stretch out and compress itself in a thousand melodic ways. Months on end may pass blindingly in a quick series of chords, open-shut, together-apart; and then a single melancholy week may seem like a year's pining, one long unfolding note.

Time seems to move at a different pace, even though we know that the clock ticks on at exactly the same rate. Indeed, the clock is a machine designed to do exactly that. In contemporary industrial societies, our lives are so organized around clock time that we get lost without a timepiece—we don't know when to eat, go to bed, meet friends, catch a bus, show up for work, or get up in the morning. Yet clock time is a relatively recent development in human experience. A theoretical reflection on time reminds us of how something that seems so natural is actually a social construction reflecting a particular hierarchical organization of human affairs. It also ties the rise of the clock to the idea of change over time, to the historical character of human experience.

THE RISE OF THE CLOCK

T HE DANISH writer Peter Høeg offers a fascinating exploration of the meanings of time in his novel *Borderliners*. Time
is central to this story about a few "problem" kids who are
taken into a prestigious school as a grand experiment by the
ambitious headmaster Biehl, who believes he has figured out
the correct methods to tame the human spirit. At the core of
this process of domestication is punctuality, life by the clock
and the timed bell. The combination of the bells and the headmaster's watch "saturated the school with a finely meshed
web of time" (Høeg 1995, 68).

This web of time is central to the project of taming spirits,
capturing individuals within the imposed order of the school
as surely as a net traps a wild animal. Those of us who have
been raised in a culture organized around clock time take our
captivity in the web of time for granted. Høeg reminds us that
there is nothing natural about this process.

For most of human history, people experienced time in
terms of natural cycles. They organized their work and leisure, sleep and waking, on the basis of the daily cycle of light
and dark, the annual cycle of the seasons, and the great cycle
of life and death. Clock time replaces nature's cycle with a
timeline in which everything is organized chronologically as a
single story of past, present, and future.

The invention of the mechanical clock did not immediately
change the cyclical rhythm of life. Høeg suggests that the
clock was not developed initially as a useful tool but rather
as a technical marvel. The presence of a mechanical clock in
the town square had little impact on the lives of most people,
who still lived their lives according to the rhythm of natural
cycles:

> What fascinated people about the measurement of time
> was not time itself, because that was dictated by other
> factors.
> What fascinated them was the clock. (Høeg 1995, 64)

The clock itself was fascinating because it represented the workings of the universe in a new way. It was, therefore, "like a work of art, a product of the laboratory, a question." It represented a challenge, a puzzle, a symbol of great unknowable natural forces. But this changed. "The clock has stopped being a question. Instead it has become the answer" (Høeg 1995, 64). Clock time becomes the answer to the taming of the human spirit.

Høeg's novel explores the use of time, focusing on a fictitious school called Biehl's Academy. The story is narrated by the central character, who is one of the "problem" students in the school. He rebels in the end, using his resources to break out of the web of time and escape the discipline of the school. As he does so, he reflects on how the school is organized around time. His analysis of the role of time becomes crucial as he tries to make sense of his own experiences inside the school and his escape from it. He eventually concludes that the school is a massive experiment in the use of time management to tame the human spirit.

> I believe that Biehl's Academy was the last possible point in three hundred years of scientific development. At that place only linear time was permitted, all life and teaching at the school was arranged in accordance with this—the school buildings, environment, teachers, pupils, kitchens, plants, equipment, and everyday life were a mobile machine, a symbol of linear time. (Høeg 1995, 260–61)

In fact, Biehl's Academy is rather typical of the places that Erving Goffman (1961) designated as "total institutions," such as prisons, the military, and psychiatric hospitals. These institutions aim to remake the individual through microscopic regulation that completely transforms her or his relationship with the world. One of the central features of these total institutions is an absolutely rigid timetable that minutely controls the individual's life rhythms.

Timetabling is not, however, unique to total institutions in the contemporary world. Being on time is a central feature of contemporary urban life, shaping our experience of the workplace, the school, and the home, as well as many of our leisure activities. Time has been quantified and standardized. Clark Blaise (2000, 5) suggests that the development of standard time, a unified system of time measurement on a global scale, "is the ultimate expression of human control over the apparently random forces of nature." It is also the ultimate expression of the control of some humans over others.

E.P. Thompson argues that the increased dominance of clock time was related to new forms of discipline associated with capitalist work relations, which regulated work by the clock rather than by the amount of time required to complete a task:

> Those who are employed experience a distinction between their employer's time and their "own" time. And the employer must *use* the time of his labour, and see it is not wasted: not the task but the value of time when reduced to money is dominant. Time is now currency: it is not passed but spent. (Thompson 1993, 359)

Thus, the modern factory system was oriented around clock time. The operation of the factory was organized around workers who showed up at the same moment and worked until the end of their shifts. Before most individuals had their own watches or clocks, the factory bell was introduced to summon workers to their shifts; the school bell was developed soon after to introduce children to the regime of **time-discipline**.

Thompson argues that time-discipline was a specific strategy developed by employers to regulate the activities of working people rather than a general necessity in a complex industrial society. Workers initially resisted this new regime of time-discipline, and it often took generations before it began to seem normal. Workers were used to living their lives according to different rhythms that seemed more natural and more autonomous, and they did not take easily to being governed by the clock (see Thompson 1993, 394).

The historical development of time-discipline is relived biographically in every generation as parents try to get kids to go to bed at a specified hour or ready for school or day care in the morning. Children live in a land before time. For children, time is qualitative and non-standardized, as they make clear when adults try to tell them that time is up for an activity they are enjoying. Children want to eat when they desire food and to do any activity only as long as it is engaging: "Are we there yet?" they cry.

Parents introduce children to time-discipline, preparing them for a society organized around clock time. Over the past 30 years, the organization of children's lives around clock time has become considerably more rigid as employed parents have become busier and attitudes have shifted to favour structured activities over free play (see Sears 2003, Chapter 7).

THE GREAT SPEED-UP

W E HAVE all become rather more bound up in the web of time because of the contemporary condition of "speed-up." Science writer James Gleick (1999) makes an interesting case that the experience of time has accelerated because of technological innovation, particularly in the areas of communications and transportation. Humans can now communicate instantly across the vastest distances and move through space at a speed earlier generations could not have imagined. Electric light breaks the barrier of night while mechanical heating and cooling reduce the impact of the seasons except in specific areas of activity (such as farming or landscaping). The rhythms of life are increasingly detached from the cycles of nature and reoriented around the movements of the clock.

These movements of the clock have become ever more precise as technology has advanced, so that the seconds that were once regarded as a tiny measure are now broken up into thousands of units. As minuscule measures of time (nanoseconds) become meaningful, we can scrutinize time use much more closely. As Gleick (1999, 6) writes, "We have reached the epoch of the nanosecond. This is the heyday of speed."

We who are living in this speed-up hardly notice it. Theoretical analysis allows us to reflect on this experience and ask questions about things that we usually do without thinking. It is not enough, however, to identify a speed-up; we must seek an explanation for it. As with our assessment of the effects of the invention of the clock, we are setting aside the technological explanation that scientific advances in themselves account for the experience of speed-up. Rather, we want to relate speed-up to changes in the social arrangements between people.

A provocative discussion of the phenomenon of speed-up can be found in the work of Karl Marx. According to Marx, one of the defining characteristics of capitalist societies is the importance of ongoing market exchange. As more and more human products become commodities, things or services are made to be exchanged on the market. A generation ago, water was generally treated as a public utility in Canada and the United States. Now it is increasingly a commodity, bottled for sale in the corner store or sold by competing vendors to individual consumers.

The orientation of products towards the market has important implications for the experience of time. Marx (1977) argues in *Capital* that the market value of commodities is not arbitrary but based on the quantity of the one specific ingredient they all contain: a given quantity of labour, even if that is not listed in the ingredients on the side of the package. The way to value a car against a house or a ton of rice is to measure the amount of this one common ingredient in all of them: labour measured in units of time.

Corporations, then, gain a competitive advantage by minimizing the amount of labour time that is contained in a particular commodity. The product containing the least labour time can generally be sold for the cheapest price. Consequently, corporations have invested tremendous resources to reduce the amount of labour time contained in their products. Indeed, the whole system of scientific management associated with mass production focuses on minimizing the labour time contained in products by minutely regulating the way workers spend their time on the job.

Frederick Taylor was a pioneer in the development of scientific management around the end of the nineteenth century and the beginning of the twentieth. The social critic Harry Braverman (1974, 90) argues that the central thrust of Taylor's innovations was to dramatically increase management control over workers' moment-to-moment activities. Management was to acquire systematic knowledge of the labour process and use it to control every aspect of work by the assembly-line method of breaking the whole operation into discrete tasks and establishing specific routines for the completion of each task. These routines were established using time and motion studies in which the precise movements of the worker's body were documented and correlated to the detailed measurement of time required to complete tasks.

Scientific management was founded on the idea of speed-up. This idea has become a taken-for-granted feature of our modern life. As a later section explores in greater detail, over the last 30 years, speed-up has led to a tremendous time squeeze that hits women most directly, given that they tend to bear the greatest responsibility for unpaid housework—rearing children, cooking and cleaning, caring for aging relatives, shopping, and all the other activities that keep a household running—even when women are employed outside the home. Cutbacks in health and social services are making these duties even more onerous now. A study of the households of Hamilton steelworkers, for example, shows that women consistently do more housework than their spouses, in most cases at least double the amount (Livingstone and Asner 1996, 86–87). The combination of work, housework, and school leaves many of us overworked and starved for time.

Clock time seems as natural as the sunrise when you have organized your life around it. But the predominance of clock time is the product of very specific changes in social relations over the past 200 years. A timeline plotting the historical changes in time use helps us step back from something that seems very obvious in the contemporary context to see how it got to be that way. In the next section, we will look specifically at the importance of historical notions of change over time in our understanding of the world around us.

TIMELINES

IN OUR theory classes, we often refer to historical events to establish a context in which to understand the development of particular theoretical schools. We often sense a groan in the class when we shift over to historical topics. Alan imagines at least some of the students rolling their eyes and saying to themselves, "Back in the day, when this professor was young and Rome was still an empire. . . ."

Many people seem to think that they do not need to know much about history to understand the world. In this section, we're going to try to persuade you that an **historical imagination** is absolutely essential to understanding our present society. We begin with the simplest idea: we cannot know the future. It is impossible to know what will happen in the next minute, let alone in days, weeks, or years.

We cannot know the future, yet we usually try to live every day as if we do. We make arrangements assuming that the sun will rise, the buses will run, and the people we treasure will be where we expect them to be when we expect them to be there. We act as if we know the future by making predictions based on the past.

In fact, all of our assumptions about the future are drawn from the past. It is only because these things have happened that we assume they will continue to happen. We generalize from the patterns of the past to generate expectations of the future. So the only reliable information we have on the future is historical.

How do you decide what to pack for a weekend trip? You might check the weather report, but you can never really trust the long-term forecasts. Mainly, you rely on past experiences. The place you are visiting at that time of year is likely to be warm or cold; you are likely to need to dress up for a celebratory event or not. Alan always packs an extra pair of pants because, on one weekend trip, it poured rain. His pants got soaked, and he didn't have another pair with him. No one else had pants that fit him, so he had to sit around in a pair of borrowed pants that made him look ridiculous. Now he knows that it is a false economy to save weight in his luggage by counting on wearing only the pants he has on; the weekend could include pouring rain and wet pants.

One of the things we all do as we get to know someone new is to find out what we can about that person's past. For example, if you are considering a relationship with someone, it is interesting to find out a bit about that person's previous patterns of interaction. Has she left a trail of broken hearts? Has he ever had a relationship that lasted? Has she ever been single?

Pretty much any personal counselling you receive will involve some sort of discussion of your past. The classic version of Freudian psychotherapy is based on the strong conviction that you need to understand when and how particular patterns in your life were established. The answer to problems with commitment, procrastination, or gambling addiction you now face lie somewhere in the past—when you established these patterns. The problem is that we are not fully conscious of the process through which our various patterns of living were established.

This biographical pattern of understanding the present and the future by understanding the past also applies to our examination of social relations. We need to understand how things got to be this way if we are to understand the way we live now and the possibilities for the future. James Baldwin (1985, 410) expresses this brilliantly:

> History, as nearly no one seems to know, is not merely something to be read. And it does not refer merely, or even principally, to the past. On the contrary, the great force of history comes from the fact that we carry it within us, are unconsciously controlled by it in many ways, and history is literally present in all we do.

To put it starkly: the past is present. At the individual level, we understand fairly easily that we carry our history inside us and that it is present in the things we do. The hurts and triumphs of our past shape our feelings, expectations, knowledge, and motivations for what lies ahead. One of us grew up excelling at sports and foolishly assumed that everyone did, but the other was humiliated by his performance in high school gym class and tried to avoid anything that smelled of sports for a long time after that. A friend of ours assumed he could not do well in school, in part because of a teacher who made fun of him in front of his class for spelling badly. Some people end up reliving the patterns of their parents' relationships while others dedicate themselves to trying to do the opposite. These actions are not necessarily conscious or intended.

The same thing happens at the level of society. Our life course is framed by the historical development of the society we live in. Our present world is the product of wars, natural disasters, cultural developments, specific forms of inequality, economic boom and bust, and the movement of peoples. Our standard of living; our expectations of school, work, and leisure; and our social relationships are all the result of events in the past. It matters in the automotive industry that workers unionized through very difficult struggles in the 1930s and 1940s. Similarly, the pattern of work in the Canadian retail sector depends, in part, on failed union drives or strikes at the Eaton's chain of stores in the 1940s and 1980s.

As we become conscious of the ways the past has shaped the present, we gain the capacity to shape the future. The problem is that we live in the present and are often not conscious of how things got to be this way. We begin with the results of the long process of historical development before our eyes. Once a building is built, the whole process of construction is hidden from us; we cannot see the foundations, the girders that support the structure, or the pipes and wires that line the insides. The same is true for our vision of society:

> Reflection on the forms of human life, hence also scientific
> analysis of these forms, takes a course directly opposite to

> their real development. Reflection begins *post festum* [after
> the feast], and therefore with the results of the process of
> development ready to hand. (Marx 1977, 168)

Our understanding of society and of our own lives is necessarily retrospective. We look back from the present, which
is the latest moment in the process of development. We can
understand the world around us only by asking how it got to
be this way. The influential nineteenth-century French sociologist Émile Durkheim states, "there is no sociology worthy of
the name that does not possess a historical character" (quoted
in Frisby and Sayer 1986, 40–41).

C. Wright Mills argues that the great promise of social science is that it might help people develop their own capacities
for the "sociological imagination," a way of seeing the world
that allows individuals to understand their place within larger
historical and social processes. He writes, "the individual can
understand his own experience and gauge his own fate only
by locating himself within his period" (Mills 1959, 5). This
sociological imagination allows people to see how their own
activity matters:

> By the fact of his living he contributes, however minutely,
> to the shaping of this society and to the course of its
> history, even as he is made by society and by its historical
> push and shove. (Mills 1959, 6)

The sociological imagination allows us to understand not
only the forces that shape our world but also the potential
for our own activity to change it. Mills argues strongly that
an historical vision is absolutely central to this endeavour.
Once we see particular forms of social inequality as the
product of particular historical developments, for example,
we can begin to understand what kind of remedy might
be necessary. James Baldwin (1985, 411) writes that white
Americans, in his experience, deny responsibility for racism
and structural inequality in dialogue with African Americans,
saying, "Do not blame me. I was not there." A genuinely

historical vision challenges us to remember that the past is not simply behind us; it is inside us in ways we often do not recognize.

Thinking Point: Your Own Historical Imagination

It is fairly easy to see on a personal scale that it matters how you got to where you are today. A person who has decided to undertake a postsecondary education after many years of full-time employment will see the classroom differently than a student arriving directly out of high school. Your sense of yourself in education is shaped by your triumph over the guidance counsellor who told you that you would never make it to university, by your glorious "A" average in Grade 10, or by resisting the father who insisted that you had to study accounting as he had. You might have moved from a tiny town to be in a larger urban centre or stayed at home where you have always lived.

It can be more difficult to imagine how larger historical processes, particularly those outside of your own experience, have shaped the way you live today. The things you read in history books or see in museums may seem to be very removed from your own experience. A documentary film might bring history to life a bit more but still not address the gap between the past and the life you live now.

However, the historical process that has led up to this moment has had a huge impact on the way you live. The education, jobs, health care, or leisure activities that are available to you now frame your expectations of life in ways you might not realize. It is quite a different experience, for example, to come to terms with being lesbian or gay at a time when at least some of your basic rights have been recognized than it would have been in the 1950s or 1960s.

One of the best ways to find some sort of bridge between historical events and your own experience is to begin to investigate relatively recent occurrences—a big rock concert, a major sports triumph, an important strike, an election, an assassination, or a war—and speak to someone who was there. It makes a big difference hearing about such an event from someone who was there and then asking the questions you need to ask to understand it. Can you think of a time someone told you a story that made the experience of a time and place far removed seem very vivid? How did that experience affect you? What did you learn from it?

The aim, over time, is to be able to hone your imagination so that you begin to see, or at least wonder about, the past as it is still here with us. You ask what the original purpose of an older building was, or who used to live in a particular house, or why there are still cottages inside the park. Rather than simply being satisfied or dissatisfied with the education you receive, you might ask how it evolved. Universities, for example, developed as a form of elite education and have only more recently become accessible to people from a wider range of backgrounds. How much has that long history of elite education shaped the postsecondary experience of today? Understanding the university's historical development will help clarify what kind of changes might be possible and how they might be accomplished. Imagine that 20 years from now, a new student movement created a much healthier and more effective system of postsecondary education. What would the new universities look like? How, specifically, would they be different from the schools of today? What are the key obstacles that currently exist preventing your imagined system from taking shape?

WHOSE HISTORY?

THE SOCIOLOGICAL imagination, then, is the capacity to understand the influence of past development on our present activities and on what might be possible in the future. It is a crucial dimension of theoretical thinking, as it enables us to understand the forces that have shaped the world presented to our senses. The development of a historical vision as part of the sociological imagination is not simply a question of amassing facts about the past.

The reconstruction of the past is never a neutral activity; it is always done from some point of view, whether conscious or unconscious. You look at a photograph of yourself with a lover, for example, quite differently when the relationship is going well and after you have broken up. The story of how we came here looks different depending on the perspective of the teller.

In society, it is the powerful who most often control the reconstruction of the past. Most of us learn history through official versions taught in schools, remembered in monuments, presented in museums, or shown in movies or on television. Official versions of history tend to be guided by the assumptions of social order theory. This means that they view the society we now live in as being the highest point in a long historical process of human development. According to social order theory, the general tendency throughout history has been one of improvement and innovation, even if, at times, the pace of change has been extremely slow. For example, social order theorists would point out that it took a long time for the idea of democracy to triumph, as it required a sufficiently open society for the interchange of discussion and debate to thrive, and these conditions took centuries to evolve. After long periods of relatively little social change, the rise of contemporary industrial society finally cast aside the despotism of rule by the nobility allied with a single official religion, bringing to the fore a new kind of leadership based on achievement rather than ascription. As a result, according to social order theory, people now have access to better and better knowledge of the world and are therefore able to improve society. We can round out this brief sketch of a social order model of history by noting that the current stage of globalization is viewed from this perspective as a crucial one in the spread of modern industrial society around the world, as the stage during which ongoing prosperity will reach the whole population of the planet. Social order theory is optimistic about ongoing improvement, seeing the free exchange of goods and ideas as providing us with the basis for meeting the challenges we face in continuing the progress towards prosperity and the good life that we have made so far.

The conflict theorist Eric Hobsbawm (1983) describes the development of these official versions of national history as the "invention of traditions." He argues that national governments got heavily into the business of developing an official version of the past in the face of militant working-class activism at the end of the nineteenth and beginning of the twentieth centuries. These official versions drew heavily on invented traditions that clothed emerging patterns of social organization in the garb of historical continuity and heritage.

This perception of historical continuity is particularly important to help maintain the power of the elite in the context of a capitalist society. Capitalism is a very disruptive social system, constantly reinventing itself with new technologies, work organization, and political conflicts. Firms grow or wither, countries prosper or suffer, empires wax or wane. Marx captures this disruptive character of capitalism quite poetically in *The Communist Manifesto*:

> All fixed, fast-frozen relations, with their train of ancient
> and venerable prejudices and opinions, are swept away,
> all new-formed ones become antiquated before they can
> ossify. All that is solid melts into air. (Marx 1969, 111)

This disruption generally serves corporations well. Employers want to shake up the workplace to drive up productivity and are not satisfied with the response that this is the way we have always done things. Products are sold as "new," "improved," even "revolutionary." But this disruption also poses a problem as those in power seek to maintain their positions. They might want to revolutionize our taste in underarm deodorants, but they also want us to respect the authority of the employer, the laws, the police, the politicians, and the bureaucrats. The invention of traditions contributes to people's respect for authority by constructing a version of the past that legitimates the present.

These invented traditions tend to make people more conservative, binding them to the way things are. The official version of history presents one's own country's military activity as always peacemaking, liberating, or defensive while that of the other side is cast as warmongering, repressive, and aggressive. The standard version of world history we learn in North American schools tends to justify an oppressive world order by reflecting a European perspective. The peoples of Africa, the Americas, Asia, or Australia are presented as "without a history" until they enter the story when they are colonized by Europeans (Wolf 1982).

As a result of what they learn in school, people of European ancestry tend to acquire ethnocentric ideas of cultural superiority. These ideas are often cleansed of the nastiest sorts of racism, yet they carry with them assumptions about who makes things happen in history and whose culture and science matter. Baldwin (1985, 410) argues that this produces an acceptance of the way things are and an inability to change:

> . . . people who imagine that history flatters them (as it does, indeed, since they wrote it) are impaled on their history like a butterfly on a pin, and become incapable of seeing or changing themselves or their world.

Movements of the disadvantaged challenge these official histories as they gain momentum. The social movements of the 1960s, for example, unleashed a whole wave of histories from the perspective of women, workers, people of colour, and lesbians and gays. The stories of those "hidden from history" provide an important source of pride and help disadvantaged people develop a sense of their capacity to change the world (see Rowbotham 1973; Duberman, Vicinus, and Chauncey 1989). Baldwin argues that there was an important historical dimension to his own process of becoming an advocate of freedom for African Americans: "I am speaking as an historical creation which has had to bitterly contest its history, wrestle with it, and finally accept it in order to bring myself out of it" (Baldwin 1985, 410).

History courses in most schools, for example, don't expose students to the history of North America from the perspective of the First Nations people who lived here when the Europeans arrived. It is true that the absolute omission of Aboriginal peoples has now generally been corrected, so students no longer read about explorers entering the empty lands, sometimes guided by mysterious natives. But it is not enough to tell the story of the subjugation of Aboriginal peoples from a European perspective, one that makes this conquest sound like an inevitable cost of progress. Histories of the world expand substantially with the inclusion of some sense of the ways of life of Aboriginal peoples, their experience of conquest, and the deliberate destruction of their culture over time. The unsettling experience of rethinking the conquest of North America from First Nations' perspectives necessarily raises important issues about the legitimacy of European domination and the claims of the nation-states produced through that historical process of subjugation.

The Idle No More movement for Indigenous sovereignty argues that decolonization also involves changes to how time itself is widely conceived and lived. At the height of the Idle No More protests of 2013, Douglas Sanderson (2013), a University of Toronto law professor and a member of the Opaskwayak Cree Nation wrote the following:

> Time [...] is on our side, because, in at least some of our languages, time is circular, not linear and so we aren't racing against a clock, we are where we will be again, and where we have been before. In the Blackfoot language there is a word for today, tomorrow and the day after tomorrow, and then yesterday, and the day before yesterday. After that, the word for three days from now, and three days in the past is the same word. Time turns in on itself. Everything that will ever happen will happen in the next two days, and the ancient ancestors are themselves only three days into the past. Thus, in Blackfoot, the stories that are told are not ancient stories, they are recent history, and their teachings are contemporary.

The Haudenosaunee nations are guided by the "Seventh Generation" principle, which requires people to consider how the decisions of today will affect "those who are not yet born but who will inherit the world" (Haudenosaunee Confederacy n.d.). In contrast to the conceptions of time deeply shaped by capitalism's never-ending competition for profit accumulation, the Seventh Generation principle instructs decision makers "to respect the world in which they live as they are borrowing it from future generations." Struggles over how time is understood and organized amount to much more than academic navel-gazing; they have the power to help protect or destroy life on Earth.

TIME MACHINE

H.G. WELLS'S novel *The Time Machine*, published in 1895, explores the idea of travel through time. The main character in the novel, the Time Traveller, claims that it is as possible to move through time as through space, except that humans have not yet invented the means. At some level, he claims, we all time travel:

> For instance, if I am recalling an incident very vividly I go back to the instant of its occurrence: I become absentminded, as you say. I jump back a moment. Of course, we have no means of staying back for any length of Time, any more than a savage or an animal has of staying six feet above the ground. (Wells 1983, 24)

The actual description of time travel in the book is quite vivid. As time accelerates, objects lose their solidity and liquify: "The whole surface of the earth seemed changed— melting and flowing under my eyes" (Wells 1983, 37).

We have moved no closer to implementing time travel in the years since Wells wrote his book, but we do know more clearly now through the refinement of atomic theories that everything that seems solid is, in fact, in motion. The tabletop that appears so sturdy and fixed when you hit it is nothing but an arrangement of whirring atomic particles in constant motion.

The sociological imagination grounded in historical vision is crucial to our ability to recognize the relationship between solidity and movement at the scale of society. We cannot travel through time physically (except in one direction at a given pace), but we must do so intellectually through the activity of reconstructing the past if we hope to understand the present and gain some control over the future. It is only this historical vision, for example, that allows us to see that time itself is a social construction and not simply a natural phenomenon.

TIME FOR DEMOCRACY?

BECAUSE TIME is a social construction, it has been experienced differently during different historical periods. And, although capitalist societies have always involved some degree of social speed-up, the Marxist geographer David Harvey (1990) argues that time has been accelerating faster than ever since the early 1970s. In his book *The Condition of Postmodernity*, Harvey (1990, 286) explains that developments in the ways in which goods and services are produced, traded, and consumed have led the world to become dominated by "the values and virtues of instantaneity . . . and disposability." Look around you and it will not be difficult to see the truth in what Harvey suggests about life today. Think about how irritating it can be when the computer takes more than half a second to move between web pages! In the words of Rosa and Scheuerman (2009, 1), "Speed dating and drive-through funerals remind us that even basic life activities appear to be speeding up: fast food, fast learning, fast love. Neighbors, fashions and lifestyles, jobs and lovers, political convictions, and even religious commitments appear to change at constantly heightened rates."

A good example of the economic practices that Harvey blames for the warp speed of the postmodern era is the increasing reliance upon methods of "just-in-time" delivery. Whereas factories used to keep most of the parts needed to build goods in warehouses at the plant, typical production processes changed in the early 1970s. Around that time, the people who owned and managed factories began trying to save money by reducing the on-site parts inventory and ordering only the precise number of parts required to meet the production goals of a particular week or even day. Harvey notes that the 1970s also saw the introduction of a variety of new forms of credit designed to allow businesses and households to access money faster. He also describes how the so-called culture industries (movies, television, art galleries, design firms, and so on) began specializing "in the acceleration of turnover time through the production and marketing of images" (Harvey 1990, 290).

According to Harvey (1990, 285), one major consequence of these changes is to "accentuate volatility" in everyday life, to make it seem as though hardly anything about social life is stable or continuous. Numerous sociologists and philosophers, notably Hermann Lubbe (2009, 158), argue that such extreme volatility is causing a "contraction of the present." Lubbe's term is meant to describe an era in which history—even recent history—seems less and less capable of informing our contemporary experiences while, at the same time, the future appears more and more unpredictable. Can you even imagine life without the Internet? But that was invented less than 20 years ago! Knowing how fast technology changes, how can we possibly expect to predict what life will look like 20 years from now? According to this view, the only thing constant is drastic and unforeseen change.

Postmodern theorists such as the ones discussed in Chapter 5 tend to celebrate these developments. Lyotard (1984), for instance, suggests that instability and rapid change liberates us from our mundane lives and fosters the exploration of our fluid identities. Harvey argues against this interpretation of the effects of postmodern speed-up. In contrast to Lyotard and other postmodernists, Harvey says that being in a state of constant flux is likely to lead to a widespread identity crisis. If people feel as though the solid ground below their feet has melted into air, then it becomes very difficult to take a firm stand on social issues. If policies, governments, jobs, and technologies are always changing, how do we know where we fit in? And how can we plan for anything—from an education to a career to a new way of organizing society—if the only thing we can be certain about is perpetual uncertainty? In an era of just-in-time delivery, or "lean production," life becomes extremely stressful, especially for workers. "The stress comes from the speed of the [assembly] line, the apparently ever-present threat of lay-offs, the minimal employment levels and the intolerance of delay built into 'just in time' societies" (Sears 2003, 8–9).

It is worthwhile to pause and think about the potential impact of an increasingly volatile sense of time on our ability to exercise the sociological imagination. In other words, if we aspire to live in a democratic society, we ought to be asking whether the acceleration that Harvey talks about limits our opportunities to participate in collective decision-making processes. Today's Western consumer culture encourages us to expect and demand everything in an instant: instant messaging, crash diets, video on demand, premade cocktails in a can. But in the words of the late French historian Jean Chesneaux (2000, 411), "There is no such thing as 'instant democracy.'" Economic exchange and consumer culture tend to be "dictated by innovation, change, and replacement through obsolescence" (Wolin 1997, 6). Democracy, by contrast, takes time. Democracy is about talking *and* listening, reflecting *and* predicting, agreeing *and* disagreeing—and that means that democracy is often messy. Even David Harvey would agree that efficiency is not a bad thing in and of itself and that there are situations in which it is essential to act without delay. Nevertheless, theoretical thinking demands that we carefully examine the social implications of postmodern speed-up—especially the extent to which the acceleration of life serves to promote or disrupt our capacity for collective action.

Thinking Point: Time Management

Teachers and employers in the twenty-first century talk a lot about the importance of "time management." They say that successful students and workers are expected to develop the skills necessary to balance multiple demands: classes, assignments, paid-work hours, and all the pressures that make up personal lives. By shedding light on how an individual's experience of the world is shaped by the ways in which time is organized by social forces, methodical inquiry usefully complicates the dominant idea that managing time is a matter of individual choices.

It's common for people in different situations to feel a general sense of busyness, boredom, or time slipping away. Less common is careful reflection on the source of these feelings beyond our own personal attitudes and states of mind. A methodical approach to the interconnections between our personal lives and the social contexts in which lives unfold has the potential not only to highlight important existing temporal patterns but also to raise questions about what it would take to reorganize time— to manage time differently—at both the micro and macro levels. Here is one way to start thinking more systematically about the relationships tying together time management, health, happiness, and power:

Step 1. Chart your next week hour by hour, breaking down what you are doing for each hour span. Of course, some hours you do more than one thing, so try to name the activity that most shaped the hour. Try simply to describe the activity you undertook hour by hour

Step 2. Look over the chart you've made and distinguish between *free time* and *controlled time*:
- Use a simple code (for example, FT/CT or a colour scheme) to mark off the different periods of your week.
- It might be interesting to note whether you've come up with a working definition of free and controlled time and how yours compares with others'.

Step 3. Make a few comments about how the balance of your actual time as represented in the chart compares with your ideal balance (that is, the way you'd balance your time if it were all up to you).

Step 4. Make a list of things that would need to change at both the micro and macro level in order to move from the actual state of things closer to your ideal.

Does this brief inquiry into your own experience suggest anything about broader relationships among time management, health, happiness, and power?

8

Conclusion: The Politics of Social Theory

THEORETICAL THINKING provides useful tools for making sense of the world around us. It allows us to press beyond what we think we already know about our environment, putting aside the fear of sounding silly and asking the most naïve questions about the way things work. The preceding four chapters have taken apart familiar concepts (the classroom, reality, nature, and time) to demonstrate the ways that theoretical thinking within a methodical process of inquiry can reframe our understanding of reality.

We have not yet penetrated very far into the tangled forest of formal theories that influence scholarly work in the humanities and social sciences. This forest can seem dense and forbidding, as these formal theories appear to us as a set of schools, overgrown and twisted together in endless debates. It can be very difficult to find a way in, to recognize where one tree ends and another begins.

This book recommends a method of tracing each tree back to the ground, identifying how it is rooted in a few key premises. The previous chapters have given you some experience in that method, using debates among social order, conflict, and postmodern perspectives as a recurring example. The book also recognizes the tendency of Indigenous ways of knowing to trouble all three of these core social sciences and humanities frameworks. Our approach, then, has provided you with a limited experience of engagement with formal theory, but there are many more debates and models lurking in the woods.

This final chapter builds on the ideas about methodical inquiry introduced in Chapters 2 and 3 to equip you a bit better for your engagement with the schools of formal theory that frame contemporary theoretical thinking. Specifically, we will examine the debate between those who argue that theory is a neutral tool for understanding the world and those who see it as a guide to action for social change. This debate offers some important insights into the divergent approaches to theorizing that make this area of study so contentious.

Finally, we will return to the conflict, social order, and postmodern models to emphasize how formal theoretical analysis flows from central premises. It really helps, when trying to make sense of theory, to develop your own compass that allows you to read theory in relation to a few fixed reference points derived from key debates. You will find it easier to understand the ideas you encounter if you aim to be consciously methodical and reflective when inquiring into the inquiry of others. If you can begin to classify theories as you read them as conflict, social order, postmodern, or none of the above, you will be better able to make sense of the logic that links the various points each theory makes.

CAN'T WE ALL GET ALONG?

IT CAN be very difficult to figure your way into the existing bodies of theory that one faces in the social sciences and humanities. They often seem to be very far removed from reality and so highly worked out as to be untouchable. Further, it can be a bit like stepping into a family feud where everyone wants you to pick a side, and you can't understand what the argument is all about.

We believe that the most fruitful approach to making sense of these debates is to try to understand the core assumptions about human nature, the way we know, or the character of the world that serve as a foundation for every major body of theory. The key premises of the conflict theory, for example, lead to a very different vision of globalization than those of the social order model. If you simply learn the fact that a conflict model theorist said one thing about globalization and a social order theorist said the opposite, you would still not have identified the core logic that links the perspective on globalization back to the cornerstone of the theory. Similarly, although not all postmodern theorists will say exactly the same thing about globalization, their critiques of both social order and conflict theory on the matter will share some basic assumptions. Theories are far clearer when you understand that each rests on a key foundation that determines the shape of the whole structure.

It would be much easier if there were only one theory. Not that long ago, in the discipline of sociology, a thinker named Talcott Parsons (1968) set out to develop the "one big theory" that would unite the discipline. Parsons saw himself as performing a great synthesis, as weaving together the threads of all the best social theories that had emerged in Europe in the nineteenth and early twentieth centuries.

The two towering European theorists Parsons based his work on were Max Weber and Émile Durkheim. Weber focused on the study of purposeful social action, which requires an understanding of the motivations that lead people to act in certain ways. Durkheim focused on the need for moral regulation to achieve social order. Parsons brought the two together in a new theory that sought to understand the ways that our motivations are tied into the normative environment, so that our sense of why we do what we do is always connected to the broader values in our society (see Clarke 1982, 1–3; Therborn 1976, 15–19).

Parsons argued that this synthesis was based on the identification of common elements that were already present in the work of the theorists he examined. He described the book in which he first developed this synthesis as "a study in social *theory* not *theories*. Its interest is not in the separate and discrete propositions to be found in the works of these men, but in a *single* body of systematic theoretical reasoning" (Parsons 1968, xxi). He saw this theory as the foundation upon which a truly scientific sociology could be built.

This new synthesis was introduced at a time when English-language traditions in sociology were not theoretically oriented. Parsons (1968, ix) remembered graduate studies at the renowned London School of Economics "without, as far as I can remember ever hearing the name Max Weber." The other giant of European sociology, Émile Durkheim, was known, "but the discussions were *overwhelmingly* negative."

Parsons introduced his new unified theory into a relative vacuum, and it quickly became the dominant perspective in English-language sociology. Indeed, the term "theory" was often used in the singular to indicate that there was only one perspective and that was his own. People with other theoretical perspectives were largely marginalized. This domination lasted through the 1940s and 1950s but was overturned in the 1960s. By the early 1970s, it was impossible to think in terms of a single overarching social theory rather than a series of contending theories.

The reason for this dramatic change was that the social movements of the 1960s and early 1970s opened up a whole series of political discussions and debates that could not help but have a huge influence on the social sciences. The anti-war, women's liberation, lesbian and gay, anti-racist, Québécois nationalist, Aboriginal, and Third World freedom movements had a great transformative effect. The debates that raged through society made it impossible to claim, without being challenged, that theory was simply a technical matter not open to fundamental dispute.

Parsons's single unified theory could dominate sociology only during the particular political circumstances of the Cold War period in which McCarthyism shut down many forms of dissent. McCarthy's anti-Communist witch-hunt led to the firing of some radical academics and silenced others. It was possible to agree on a single theory when only a very small range of political opinion was expressible. The protests of the 1960s blew the lid off that narrow consensus.

There are many contending theories, then, because there are different political perspectives that demand expression when we investigate the social world. It might seem as if this crowded field of theories results from the meaningless activities of too many academics in ivory towers with too little to do with their time. In fact, there are many theories because they actually matter; there are meaningful political differences between the schools of thought that dominate the social sciences and humanities. In other words, there is a **politics of social theory**, meaning that each social theory has political import and carries with it various perspectives on power: who has it, what it is, how it works, and how it should be used.

One way of understanding these debates between contending theories is to see the contrast in their approach to theory itself. Each school of thought has very different perspectives on the role of theory in our understanding of the world around us. One of the dominant perspectives in the social sciences has seen theory as neutral, as an unbiased tool for the objective examination of human circumstances. That perspective has been challenged historically both by those who see theory as an important part of the struggle for social change, an instrument for identifying injustices and clarifying strategies for combating inequities, and by those who challenge theoretical claims to neutrality and the idea that mass liberation is even possible. An examination of these differences will help identify some of the points of debate that have led to the development of contending theoretical approaches.

THEORY AS NEUTRAL

Max Weber argued strongly for a distinction between politics and science. In the realm of politics, the goal was persuasion: "When speaking in a political meeting about democracy, one does not hide one's personal standpoint; indeed, to come out clearly and take a stand is one's damn duty" (Weber 1958, 145). In contrast, the goal of science was disinterested analysis. In a dispassionate analysis of democracy, for example, "one considers its various forms, analyzes them in the way they function, determines what results for the conditions of life the one form has as compared with the other." Words are "swords against the enemy" in a political meeting, but in a scientific analysis they are "plowshares to loosen the soil of contemplative thought" (Weber 1958, 145).

Many other theorists support the distinction between politics and science proposed here by Weber. They seek to develop approaches to social science that are disengaged from the day-to-day practice of political persuasion. They claim to be able to separate facts from values in their pursuit of an accurate and unbiased way of understanding the human condition.

Émile Durkheim sought to establish the grounds for a truly objective social science in his book *The Rules of Sociological Method*. In order to accomplish this aim, Durkheim (1964, 31), who took a positivist approach to social research, argued that "All preconceptions must be eradicated." A truly objective social science must begin with facts, approached objectively through sense data. The deep understanding of society means training ourselves to become disinterested observers totally detached from the things we are investigating. Durkheim (1964, 143) wrote that his method was "dominated entirely by the idea that social facts are things and must be treated as such."

According to Durkheim, then, we must treat our social reality as a set of objects that we view from the outside with empirical rigour, as things distinct from our everyday experiences. Science must stand apart from our common-sense perspectives and develop a new set of concepts "that adequately express things as they actually are, and not as everyday life finds it useful to conceive them." Science must "dismiss all lay notions and the terms expressing them, and return to sense perception, the primary and necessary substance underlying all concepts" (Durkheim 1964, 43–44).

The goal, then, was a new kind of theoretical understanding of society that was sharply demarcated from everyday assumptions and political advocacy in order to describe or interpret the world, not to change it:

> Sociology thus understood will be neither individualistic, communistic nor socialistic in the sense commonly given to those words. On principle it will ignore these theories,

in which it could not recognize any scientific value, since they tend not to describe or interpret, but to reform, social organization. (Durkheim 1964, 142)

Theories must thus be "derived from facts and not from emotions" (Durkheim 1964, 143) so that situations can be analysed neutrally to identify the specific causes of particular effects. Value judgements must be set aside to make this neutral analysis possible. Science must be concerned "only with facts, which all have the same value and interest for us; it observes and explains, but does not judge them" (Durkheim 1964, 47). The goal of such a science was to free us from partisanship:

> The role of sociology from this point of view must properly consist in emancipating us from all parties, not to the extent of negating all doctrine, but by persuading us to assume toward these questions a special attitude that science alone can give with its direct contact with things. (Durkheim 1964, 143)

Such a science could certainly have practical implications. It would replace political advocacy inspired by particular ideals with the clinical and scientific stance of the medical doctor. Politics then becomes a technical matter, the effective diagnosis of the illness and a prescription for the correct treatment:

> The duty of the statesman is no longer to push society toward an ideal that seems attractive to him, but his role is that of the physician: he prevents the outbreak of illnesses by good hygiene, and he seeks to cure them when they have appeared. (Durkheim 1964, 75)

This view presumed that it is both possible and desirable to develop a scientific approach that is genuinely objective. For example, in the 1940s, Kingsley Davis and Wilbert E. Moore (1970, 369) developed an analysis of social inequality or stratification that suggested it was a universal feature of human society that served to motivate people "to instill in the proper individuals the desire to fill certain positions, and, once in these positions, the desire to perform the duties attached to them." In a debate with a critic, Davis (1970, 387) argued that they were explaining stratification not justifying it: "By insinuating that we are 'justifying' such inequality, he falls into the usual error of regarding causal explanation of something as a justification of it."

The distinction between explanation and justification is central to an approach to theory that seeks to set aside value judgements and neutrally investigate the world that actually exists. Davis (1970, 391) claimed that they were not "concerned with the indefinite or utopian future but with societies as we find them." The core claim of this approach to theorizing is "just the facts." Theory offers explanations that can be defined in specific, observable terms, and then these explanations can be tested against the realities of "societies as we find them."

THEORY, FOR A CHANGE

THE POLAR opposite approach to theory explicitly rejects the goal of developing a neutral theory based on the investigation of the world as it is. Rather, taking a critical approach to social research, it aims to use theory as a guide to social action; it seeks to inform people of the workings of the world so they can act to change the world. Karl Marx (1978, 123) put this bluntly: "The philosophers have only *interpreted* the world in various ways; the point is to *change* it."

From this perspective, a genuinely neutral theory is neither possible nor desirable. Brian Fay (1975, 94) argues that this approach is "built on the explicit recognition that social theory is interconnected with social practice." For instance, we find it hard to read the Davis and Moore theory that stratification motivates people without thinking of contemporary debates about social welfare programs, minimum wage levels, and security of employment. There are many on the right wing of the political spectrum today who support measures that increase the gap between rich and poor on the basis that it contributes to motivation for productivity. From our perspective, it is difficult to read this theory as neutral when it seems so clearly to relate to contemporary debates. At the same time, others reply that we can all benefit from a clear, disinterested analysis of our world.

Indeed, even the way Davis and Moore framed their claim for neutrality was politically charged. The assumption that we should exclude "the indefinite or utopian future" and focus on "societies as we find them" frames our understanding of the human condition within the limits of the way things are within the actual social relations of the contemporary world. Rather than examining how things got to be this way and how they might be different, it focuses our investigation on the way things work right now. We naturalize and eternalize by generalizing about the human condition from the way people act in particular circumstances within a specific social order.

In contrast, a theory oriented to social change examines the current state of society to see how inequality and injustice might be addressed through social action by those who are subordinated, who have a disadvantaged position inside dominant power relations: "A critical social theory is meant to inform and guide the activities of a class of dissatisfied actors" (Fay 1975, 97). In this view, theory can never be neutral because it is always understood in the context of social action to shape the future of society.

Think back to Durkheim's call for a strict distinction between social scientific and everyday understandings of the world. In contrast, the theory for social change begins with the actual knowledge of those who are subordinated. As Nancy Hartsock (1998, 222) argues, "We need a theory of power that recognizes that our practical daily activity contains an understanding of the world—subjugated perhaps, but present." According to this perspective, then, the everyday theorizing we all do represents an important point of departure, not an impediment to understanding that is to be set aside.

At the same time, this theory is often not adequate in itself as it is based solely on the narrow parameters of our personal experience. As well, it is often affected by the dominant power relations in ways we do not consciously perceive. The power relations we live with day to day become integrated into our understanding of the way things work, so we simply take for granted that the boss rules in the workplace and the teacher in the classroom. Our sense of what is possible is defined in relation to those apparently fixed points on our horizons. In other words, our common-sense perspective often takes our place in the world for granted.

Theory for social change needs to go beyond that, pointing to the possibilities for freedom that are often difficult to see in the light of actual inequalities. For example, because of the restrictions workers and women experience daily, they can have trouble seeing beyond the power relations that currently structure the workplace or imagining a just division of labour between men and women. Yet they do often have a sharp view of the inequities and daily operations of the current social order. Hartsock (1998, 223) therefore suggests a two-pronged approach: "The critical steps are, first, using what we know about our lives as a basis for the critique of the dominant culture and, second, creating alternatives." There is a need for deeper theoretical work to uncover the workings of the system that are not immediately visible, even from below.

This deeper theoretical work is not simply the property of specialized theorists with lots of formal education. People engaged in trying to change the world through movements of the disadvantaged often engage actively in the analysis of their social environment. This engagement often includes encounters with formal theory such as Marxism and feminism through various educational activities ranging from study circles to cultural presentations.

The perspective of subordinated peoples provides a privileged, though partial, viewpoint that offers crucial insights into the workings of an unequal social order. According to

Hartsock (1998, 107), "women's lives make available a particular and privileged vantage point on male supremacy." The powerful have a uniquely partial perspective on the way the system operates because it generally seems to work pretty well for them. A man in a heterosexual couple, for example, might think he is carrying his share of the burden of housework if he puts his clothes in the laundry hamper rather than throwing them on the floor. A woman, on the other hand, might see what a small proportion of the everyday burden that little gesture represents because she knows through her everyday experience that the heavy work of laundry is not getting the clothes into the hamper but sorting the loads, washing, drying, folding, ironing, and putting away. The less powerful actually see more of the way the whole system works than the privileged, who tend to take for granted that this is the way things are. The world really does look different through the window of a luxury car.

Those social scientists who think of themselves as strictly neutral might not be aware of the ways that dominant perspectives are integrated into their investigation of the world. In contrast, those who use theory for social change bluntly declare their perspectives and do not claim to be impartial. However, if this theory is to lead to genuine change, its actual fit with the world is very important. The ultimate test of theory, in this case, is practice: Does applying it actually help to change the world? As Marx (1978, 121) writes, "Man must prove the truth, i.e., the reality and power . . . of his thinking in practice."

This sort of theoretical thinking requires real rigour. It is not enough to recycle biases and restate claims that have no basis in reality. "If we are to construct a more just society, we need to be assured that some systematic knowledge about our world and ourselves is possible" (Hartsock 1998, 222). This approach to systematic knowledge is, however, a very different one than that of those who regard theory as neutral and seek to describe and interpret rather than change society.

THEORY AS DECONSTRUCTION

POSTMODERN PERSPECTIVES provide a third viewpoint in debates about the role of theory. Postmodernists reject both the social order model assumption that theory should be part of a neutral social science and the conflict model assumption that theory should play a role in movements for social justice. The source of postmodern critiques of existing thought systems runs deeper than mere skepticism or even than an alternative moral code. Its criticism is rooted in its rejection of Enlightenment-inspired conceptions of reality, truth, and freedom, conceptions that inform, in varying ways, both social order and conflict theory.

When criticizing the social order model, postmodernists argue that, because all knowledge is socially constructed, there can be no such thing as objectivity or neutrality. Science (including social science), say postmodernists, is not about discovering and explaining aspects of reality that were already there. Science is about constructing the appearance of truth through existing and ever-shifting relationships of power. For example, leading scientists in the nineteenth century held that women were biologically inferior to men. According to science, women were weaker, feebler of mind, and more prone to emotional breakdown. This scientific "truth" was overturned only when the power relations associated with gender were changed throughout society. The earlier science of gender was not only wrong in its biological assumptions (despite representing itself as the undisputed facts) but helped to reproduce male domination. Science was not independent of power but inextricably bound up in it.

Postmodern perspectives assume that the interrelation between science and power can never be overcome. There is no such thing as certain knowledge; our "truths" are only different ways of representing experience. It is not as though the mistakes science once made will be eliminated as more precise tools for measurement are invented or as scientific inquiry becomes more democratic. The role of theory from the perspective of postmodernism is to critique, disrupt, interrogate, and "deconstruct" any and all claims of ultimate truth or of having access to objective reality.

It's not surprising if you've noted overlap between this aspect of postmodernism and parts of the conflict model. Certainly, conflict theory also criticizes the social order version of a neutral social science. Where postmodernism and the conflict model differ, however, is on the question of what theory ought to do instead. Conflict theory challenges the social order version of a neutral science in the name of an emancipatory vision of inquiry, one that, although dismissive of "neutrality," remains committed to discovering and explaining aspects of reality in order to find ways to achieve greater democracy and freedom. This commitment to freedom leads conflict theorists to critique existing institutions and the ways of knowing associated with them in a broader effort to discover real truths about the world—truths that foster social change.

It's this second part of the conflict model—the vision of liberation—that postmodernism rejects. In the view of postmodern theorists, because there is no such thing as universal values and because power runs in multiple directions at the same time, there can be no authentic emancipatory movement, no clear distinction between oppressive relations and freedom. Before the Soviet Union collapsed in 1989, postmodernists pointed to it as an example illustrating how the promise of mass liberation leads always to some form of totalitarianism. Postmodernists reject the universalizing character of conflict theory, for example, the way it envisions a variety of societies in terms of ruling classes and exploited classes. Instead, postmodernists emphasize the risk of cramming the multi-dimensionality of experience into great overarching categories and of focusing on the differences within social groups.

Some conflict and postmodernist theorists acknowledge that they have been influenced by each other. Some scholars, such as the Jamaican-British cultural theorist Stuart Hall, are influential in both camps. Yet, in spite of some conflict theorists becoming more sensitive to the complexity of representation and identity, and notwithstanding some postmodern theorists becoming more sensitive to the unique character of political economic pressures, serious disagreements over the role of theory continue to divide the two perspectives. Even when such debates do not erupt in open battle, there are simmering tensions beneath the surface about whether the role of theory is primarily to "deconstruct" existing knowledge systems (the postmodern perspective) or to help guide movements for liberation (the conflict perspective).

REFRAMING PROBLEMS

CERTAINLY, THIS discussion about the uses of theory does not exhaust the range of debate in the contemporary humanities and social sciences. The aim here is to provide an insight into why theoretical thinking matters. There is a sharp dispute even about the character of facts and their relationship to theory. As we have just seen, some theorists see theory as a crucial dimension in struggles to change the world while others aim for a genuinely impartial knowledge.

The impact of these differences becomes very clear if we return to the major issues discussed throughout this book. Our investigation of the classroom would look very different if it were seen to be an objective examination with an emphasis on testing observable phenomena rather than a critical analysis connected to the project of pursuing more equitable and democratic forms of education. The investigation of time is changed if one presumes it is related to domination and inequality as opposed to being a social fact to be studied in an objective manner. The idea of reality depends on whether you believe that it is a set of objects outside of us to be investigated empirically or a set of social constructions reflecting the power inequities of the society we inhabit—or that there is no such thing as reality at all. Finally, those who want to use theory to change the world try to understand how naturalization encourages resignation by making the outcome of **human agency** seem determined by natural forces. On the other hand, those committed to an objective social science begin with assumptions that the social world can be investigated in the same way one could study nature, treating historical trends as the outcome of natural laws.

You are already a theorist at some level; we all are. Yet this everyday approach to generalization will only get you so far. You can become a much sharper and more self-aware thinker by engaging with the highly developed and sometimes difficult to understand formal theories associated with academic disciplines and movements for change. Your ability to make sense of the world around you is going to matter in your life, whether you aspire to change the world or to develop neutral or disinterested insights. Theoretical explanation offers a certain command over things that you do not have if you simply accept that the way things work is a mystery.

Take the issue of student debt. If you're currently enrolled in college or university, chances are you've got a pile of it. At one level, you're facing or will soon face the problem of how to pay back your loans. Because friends have their own loans to pay off, jobs are scarce, your family doesn't have extra cash, and you'd rather not complain too much about your situation, you will most likely face this problem individually. You'll get a job or four, eat poorly, and put off travelling to visit your cousin for a few years.

Not paying off your loans could mean being punished harshly by the bank and the law, risking long-term trouble. Mindful of the forces bearing down on you, you might think that there's pretty good logic to the individualistic approach to solving the problem of student debt. However, using the power of theoretical thinking within a broader process of inquiry, you are able see the problem of student debt in a different light, one requiring a collective strategy rather than an individual one.

The average student graduating from a Canadian university today carries a debt of roughly $30,000. Student movements in Québec, Chile, and other parts of the world have argued that this debt is a problem not only for individual students but also for society more broadly. In Québec in 2012, hundreds of thousands of students went on strike to stop a 75 per cent tuition increase, which would have meant a new explosion of student debt. In the statement Share Our Future released by one of the main student unions coordinating the strike, education was reframed from being a relationship between an individual and a school to a relationship among all people:

> Because education is a training ground for humanity, and because humanity does not bow to economic competitiveness, we refuse to allow our schools to bend under the weight of well-stocked portfolios. Together we call for an egalitarian school system that will break down hierarchies, one that will pose a threat to all those men and women who still think they can rule over us with a free hand. (CLASSE 2012)

The Québec student strike did not result in free postsecondary education for all; but it did manage to stop the tuition hike the government had said was non-negotiable. It also used theory and action to reframe familiar ways of seeing the world—and to push back the horizons of what people assumed was possible. Theoretical thinking was crucial to building a shared understanding of education as a social issue that matters to everyone, an issue that must be understood in relation to other problems, such as Indigenous sovereignty, environmental justice, gender equity, and migrant rights.

Theory, then, enables this reframing of our experience of the world and lets us investigate the social questions that affect us both as individuals and as members of society. Why is inequality increasing? What causes violent crime? Why do wars happen? These issues affect your life, whatever perspective you take and however you choose to live it. The understanding of key theoretical debates about these topics is bound to provide you with both insights into the world around you and analytical skills that will improve the quality of your own everyday theorizing. Nevertheless, theoretical writing can be difficult to understand and can certainly be challenging to follow. There is, at least in theory, much at stake for you in these debates.

DECOLONIZING THEORY

Proponents of Indigenous ways of knowing who distinguish their approach to the world from Western traditions of scholarly inquiry make a number of unsettling observations that need to be seriously engaged as part of any genuine project of decolonization. First, Indigenous ways of knowing demonstrate that methodical inquiry rooted in empirical research and formal theorizing are not superior ways of knowing in all situations. For example, although knowledge of the present within many Indigenous communities is inseparable from relationships with people and animals no longer in this world and others who've not yet arrived, formal theory provides few clues when it comes to honouring and maintaining vibrant relationships with past and future generations. Categories such as nature and culture that are central to social theory are understood very differently (if not outright rejected) in many Indigenous traditions.

Second, the wealth and power of Western nations and the domination of Western ways of knowing have been built, in part, upon the murder, dispossession, and exploitation of Indigenous peoples around the world. Many of the great universities of North America are built on land stolen from Aboriginal peoples, lands that once saw genocides committed by white settlers. British society, with all its cultural and intellectual triumphs, flourishes today because, for centuries, it enslaved Indigenous people on different continents and plundered their resources. Israel's universities, leading institutions of research and development, are sometimes built on Palestinian land and often support the illegal ongoing occupation of Palestine.

This history does not mean that everything Indigenous is good and everything Western is bad. At times, some Indigenous peoples have committed terrible acts, and Western history is full of struggles for liberation, including solidarity struggles with anti-colonial movements. Our reason for emphasizing tensions around colonialism and Indigenous knowledge throughout the book is that, if social theory is to be a force for decolonization in the future, we need to face difficult questions about the links between particular ways of knowing and patterns of brutal aggression. Academic perspectives have often erased Indigenous ways of knowing while colonial regimes were forcibly imposing new forms of rule. We cannot simply use Western ways of knowing without understanding that history. This process itself will benefit from the sort of methodical reflection that guides the best theoretical thinking.

POLITICS AND THEORETICAL DEBATE

So where has our journey landed us? We can make a few conclusions. Social theory is highly contested. There are many theoretical positions on a particular topic because there are many different visions of the way things are and should be in our society. As discussed in the previous chapters, the debate between the social order and conflict models is a defining one that has shaped and reshaped the humanities and social sciences. The 1960s, for example, saw a sharp rise in the focus on conflict theories in disciplines ranging from history to political science, from English to philosophy. The conflict model rose to a new prominence in many places as students, radicalized by the social movements of the day, challenged their professors and demanded new approaches. Feminism, for example, entered into the academic arena because women mobilized and challenged the prevailing male-dominated approaches in almost every discipline.

You have been challenged throughout this book to identify the fundamental conflict or social order premises underlying contending positions on particular issues. This debate was chosen because it remains influential in some form or another across the range of humanities and social sciences. The analysis of this one debate also provided some experience in studying theory using a method that encourages you to seek out the founding premises of a theory and see how these are reflected in every position associated with that perspective. We will return to the social order versus conflict debate here to show how these models differ even in their fundamental approach to theory.

The foundation of the social order model is the premise that moral regulation creates the possibility for a civilized society by restraining the greedy, self-serving creature that lurks within all humans. The social institutions that shape and control us therefore act in the interest of all of us by creating a society in which orderly life is possible. Politics largely comes down to the technical question of how to solve any problems that might impede the development of shared values and thriving social institutions. Theory, then, is primarily an instrument for knowledge that can be seen as fundamentally neutral as it serves all of us by identifying with clear eyes the challenges facing our civilization.

In contrast, the conflict model is based on the premise that the existing society is structured by fundamental inequalities that create groups with conflicting interests who fight it out and produce social transformation. The social institutions that preserve the current order are therefore acting in the interests of the powerful, who benefit from the ongoing exploitation of the disadvantaged. Politics is the expression of the conflict in interests between the powerful and the subordinated groups, which mobilize to fight back. Theory is a tool in this struggle, either serving the interests of the powerful by convincing us that fundamental change is impossible or serving the interests of the disadvantaged by mapping out the possibilities for change.

The contrast between these models might indeed have implications for how theory is taught and learned. According to the social order perspective, theory is seen as fundamentally neutral, so learning it is a question of intellectual history, of understanding the process through which the leading-edge version of the best theoretical thinking developed. In so far as there is theoretical debate, it is taken as a sign of an immature science that has not yet produced the appropriate higher level theoretical synthesis—the theory that will provide a vision of the field capable of uniting us all, save for a few doubters cast to the outside.

According to the conflict model, on the other hand, debates within the realm of social theory reflect disputes between the powerful and the disadvantaged about how society should be run. In this case, learning theory is a question of providing you with some navigational tools, so you can situate yourself in these debates, which will continue as long as social inequality produces conflict. The claim that a single overarching theory could subsume these debates is ideological in the context of these conflicting interests in society.

You might, finally, want to situate this book in relation to these conflicting perspectives. There is some attempt at neutrality here in that positions from the conflict, social order, and postmodern models were stated fairly (we hope) and given roughly equal weight. Yet, the logic of the book and the approach to understanding theory it suggests are derived primarily from one of these models. The ability to figure out the underlying theoretical logic of any piece you are reading will serve you well in the study of theory and more broadly in negotiating the various forms of persuasion we all handle daily.

Glossary

A GLOSSARY is a guide to the specific and technical word usages in a particular text. One of the characteristics of methodical inquiry is precision in the use of language. In everyday conversations, people sometimes use words with only a rough understanding of their meaning. Using words casually in this way generally works fine, but it is not a sound basis for social science. In social science, terms such as class, nation, or poverty are used in very specific ways within particular theoretical frameworks. Use of both a dictionary for general reference and a glossary for a specific text is highly recommended as you develop your abilities to use terms in accordance with their precise technical meanings.

abstraction: Separating out the essential elements, the way a map, for example, highlights only the key elements of a landscape. Movement through levels of abstraction refers to our ability to zoom in (and focus on a micro level) and zoom out (and focus on a macro level) when interpreting objects and issues.

academic disciplines: Networks or schools of scholarly knowledge defined both by their field of study (that is, *what* they examine) and the methods they use to study it. For example, political science, English, biology, and sociology are different academic disciplines.

academic source: A text that meets the criteria for authority of a particular academic discipline (often established by passing review by other authorities in the field, i.e., "peer review"). Generally, these texts use citations to document rigorously the sources of all empirical data and analytical frames used within. Academic sources often address topics that are also addressed in non-academic or "popular" sources (for example, both academic journal articles and newspapers or blogs often focus on politics and pop culture), but the form and intended audience of the two types of sources is significantly different.

capitalism: An economic and social system based upon the ownership or control of key productive resources (such as factories, patents, and tools) by a relatively small number of people who profit from the labour of the majority, which is comprised of those who must sell their capacity to work for a wage in order to survive.

common sense: The shared perspective of a social group, which appears as factual because it is held in common.

conflict model: A theoretical perspective that sees ongoing conflict between dominant and subordinate groups as a crucial characteristic of societies based on inequality.

consciousness: The mental filter through which we interpret the world. Consciousness, which is both individual and social in nature, is the key to our constant classification of sensations and experiences.

critical social science: A theory of knowledge positing that humans are able to examine the real world outside their heads but that access to this world is always mediated by a person's social location and perspective.

culture: A very rich and highly contested term used to refer to the complex interchange between conscious human actors and their natural environment.

cycle of inquiry: A methodical way of seeking knowledge in which the investigator moves back and forth between research (observation) and theory (explanation).

deduction: An approach to understanding that begins with generalizations or theories and applies these to investigate specific phenomena. **Deductive** reasoning, then, moves from the general to the specific: e.g., sexism is prevalent in society, so it will be a factor in how adjudicators respond to the auditions of perspective violin students.

empirical data: Pieces of information collected through our five senses (seeing, hearing, touching, tasting, smelling); these are often called "sense data."

everyday theorizing: Developing explanations of the world around us based upon our own personal experiences and tastes, as opposed to through systematic inquiry. Everyday theorizing is essential to our personal navigation of the social world, but, alone, it is unable to support generalizations about the human condition.

fact: A thing or statement that is verifiable as it is founded on sense data.

feminism: A theoretical perspective rooted in the conflict model devoted to identifying and ending the systemic subordination of women. **Feminist** theory also supports activism in support of gender equity.

formal theories: The theoretical thinking associated with academic disciplines. Formal theories must meet certain standards, such as logical rigour, empirical soundness, conceptual rigour, and relationship to what is already known in a field.

functionalism: A theoretical perspective rooted in the social order model that aims to identify the ways institutions and practices help to preserve a well-regulated and orderly society.

historical imagination: A way of thinking that focuses on the links between the present and the past in order to reveal the ways in which history is active within our modern lives.

human agency: The ability of humans to act upon the world in order to achieve a goal.

human nature: Characteristics of humans that are thought to be universal (i.e., shared by all people) and biologically given.

Indigenous peoples: The peoples who inhabited a place prior to colonization, who therefore have unique, land-based claims to sovereignty and self-determination.

induction: An approach to understanding that begins by observing specific phenomena with the aim of building theories or forming conclusions. **Inductive** reasoning, then, moves from the specific to the general: e.g., although, over the last ten years, 20 per cent more women than men have auditioned for a master violin class, each year, at least half of the successful applicants are men; sexism is a factor in how adjudicators respond to the auditions of perspective violin students.

interpretive social science: A theory of knowledge that assumes we can only know the world subjectively, through our own processes of making sense and attaching meanings. We must therefore examine the ways in which reality is perceived through consciousness in order to study social life.

intersubjectivity: A conceptualization of the relation between people that involves the attribution of subjectivity to others, which results in empathy based on the assumption that consciousness is shared.

Marxism: A theoretical perspective rooted in the conflict model that focuses on the ways in which capitalism oppresses the vast majority of human beings. However, the aim of **Marxist** theory is not only to explain the world but to develop the knowledge necessary to overthrow capitalism and create a more just society.

methodical inquiry: A way of seeking knowledge that follows a clear plan, aims to achieve logical and conceptual rigour, and articulates both the benefits and limitations of the particular investigation being conducted.

modernity: A social science concept used to refer to both a particular historical period and the ways of knowing associated with it. Specifically, modernity refers to the period following the French Revolution (1787–99) and the emergence of industrial capitalism, especially in Europe. Modernity, or the modern period, is characterized by secular commitment and the prevailing assumption that everything is knowable through rigorous empirical inquiry and analysis. Critics from numerous perspectives have challenged the assumptions of modernism.

natural: The quality of objects and processes whose existence is not the result of human action.

naturalization: Treating the products of history and society as though they were the products of nature.

objectivity: The state or quality of being objective, which means analysing or presenting information in a disinterested and neutral way, as opposed to in a manner shaped by personal feelings or opinions.

opinion: Deeply held personal beliefs based on experience and personality but not necessarily on facts or expertise.

phenomenology: A theoretical perspective that studies the role of consciousness in structuring reality.

politics of social theory: A phrase used to point out the fact that all theoretical perspectives have their own "politics" or assumptions about where power resides, how power works, and for what purposes power should be used.

positivist social science: A theory of knowledge that presumes that theories verified through the rigorous collection of sense data are the exclusive basis for social scientific knowledge.

postmodern approaches: Theoretical perspectives that reject universal social theories (especially those associated with modernism) and focus instead on the localized play of language and symbols in constructing a fluid and unpredictable world.

power relations (or social relations): The ways in which control over key resources puts some people in positions of dominance over others.

racialize: The process through which language, history, and certain dominant assumptions come together to sustain the belief that specific visible differences in people's physical make-up (such as skin tone) create real differences in their personalities and capabilities.

reality: A concept used to refer to the state of things as they actually are, no matter how they may appear on the surface.

research methods: Tools for conducting methodical inquiry, for example, interviews, surveys, and textual analysis.

social order model: A theoretical perspective that views an orderly society as essential to regulating the naturally self-interested impulses of human beings.

social science: A specific way of knowing the human condition based upon research and theory.

speed-up: The acceleration of time resulting from changes in technology and economic relationships within a capitalist society.

standpoint: The specific location within social relations (such as class, gender, race, or sexuality) from which a person sees the world. The concept emphasizes the idea that things look different depending on where you stand in relation to systems of social power.

subjectivity: The interpretation of objects outside our heads through our own minds. Subjectivity is the personal lens through which we perceive the outside world.

theoretical pluralism: The general recognition within a field of study that there is more than one legitimate frame of analysis for research.

theoretical thinking: A way of interpreting the world that uses and develops a systematic explanation (or theory) of the people, events, actions, and objects around us.

theory: An explanation of a phenomenon that uses some sort of broader framework of understanding.

time-discipline: The ways in which our work lives and personal lives are shaped by the demands of the clock. Time-discipline is especially strict in capitalist economies, where wages paid by the owning class to workers are organized around units of time (for example, an hourly wage).

ways of knowing: The process for making sense of the world that frames particular understandings of reality; examples might include science, religious faith, or storytelling in oral traditions.

References

Alexander, Jeffrey. 1987. *Sociological Theory Since 1945*. London: Hutchinson.

Alterman, Eric. 2008. "Out of Print: The Death and Life of the American Newspaper." *The New Yorker*, March 31, 48–59.

Atwood, Margaret. 2000. *Negotiating with the Dead: A Writer on Writing*. Cambridge: Cambridge University Press.

Bailey, Gordon, and Noga Gayle. 2003. *Ideology: Structuring Identities in Contemporary Life*. Toronto: University of Toronto Press.

Baldwin, James. 1985. "White Man's Guilt." In *The Price of the Ticket: Collected Nonfiction, 1948–1985*, 409–14. New York: St. Martin's.

Balnaves, Mark, and Peter Caputi. 2001. *Introduction to Quantitative Research Methods: An Investigative Approach*. Thousand Oaks, CA: Sage.

Bannerji, Himani. 1995. *Thinking Through: Essays on Feminism, Marxism and Anti-Racism*. Toronto: Women's Press.

Baudrillard, Jean. 1983. *Simulations*. Trans. Paul Foss, Paul Patton, and Philip Beitchman. New York: Semiotext(e).

Baudrillard, Jean. 1995. *The Gulf War Did Not Take Place*. Trans. Paul Patton. Bloomington, IN: Indiana University Press.

Benjamin, Walter. 1999. *The Arcades Project*. Cambridge, MA: The Belknap Press of Harvard University Press.

Berger, John. 1972. *Ways of Seeing*. Harmondsworth, UK: Penguin Books.

Berger, Peter, and Thomas Luckmann. 1967. *The Social Construction of Reality*. Garden City, NY: Anchor.

Biro, Andrew. 2005. *Denaturalizing Ecological Politics: Alienation from Nature from Rousseau to the Frankfurt School and Beyond*. Toronto: University of Toronto Press.

Blaise, Clark. 2000. *Time Lord: The Remarkable Canadian Who Missed His Train and Changed the World*. Toronto: Vintage Canada.

Brand, Dionne. 1998. *Bread Out of Stone*. Toronto: Vintage Canada.

Brand, Dionne. 2001. *A Map to the Door of No Return*. Toronto: Doubleday.

Braverman, Harry. 1974. *Labor and Monopoly Capital: The Degradation of Work in the Twentieth Century.* New York: Monthly Review Press.

Brecht, Bertolt. 1964. *Brecht on Theatre.* Ed. and trans. John Willet. London: Methuen.

Butler, Judith. 1988. "Performative Acts and Gender Constitution: An Essay in Phenomenology and Feminist Theory." *Theatre Journal* 40 (4): 519–31. http://dx.doi.org/10.2307/3207893.

Carson, Rachel. 1962. *Silent Spring.* Boston: Houghton Mifflin.

Cather, Willa. 1993. *O Pioneers!* New York: Dover Publications.

Chakrabarty, Dipesh. 2000. *Provincializing Europe: Postcolonial Thought and Historical Difference.* Princeton, NJ: Princeton University Press.

Chesneaux, Jean. 2000. "Speed and Democracy: An Uneasy Dialogue." *Social Sciences Information/Information Sur les Sciences Sociales* 39 (3): 407–20. http://dx.doi.org/10.1177/053901800039003004.

Clarke, Simon. 1982. *Marx, Marginalism and Modern Sociology: From Adam Smith to Max Weber.* London: Macmillan.

CLASSE (Coalition large de l'association pour une solidarité syndicale étudiante). 2012. "Share Our Future: The CLASSE Manifesto." Stop the Hike. Accessed August 4, 2014. http://www.stopthehike.ca/wp-content/uploads/2012/07/Share-Our-Future-The-CLASSE-Manifesto.pdf.

Corbetta, Piergiorgio. 2003. *Social Research: Theory, Methods, and Techniques.* Trans. Berndard Patrick. Thousand Oaks, CA: Sage.

Corntassel, Jeff, Chaw-win-is, and T'lakwadzi. 2009. "Indigenous Storytelling, Truth-telling, and Community Approaches to Reconciliation." *English Studies in Canada* 35 (1): 137–59. http://dx.doi.org/10.1353/esc.0.0163.

CTV. 2007. "Debate on Black-Focused School in T.O. Gets Heated." November 27. http://toronto.ctvnews.ca/debate-on-black-focused-school-in-t-o-gets-heated-1.263520.

Daston, Lorraine, and Peter Galison. 1992. "The Image of Objectivity." *Representations* 40 (Fall): 81–128. http://dx.doi.org/10.2307/2928741.

Davis, Kingsley. 1970. "Reply." In *Readings on Social Stratification*, ed. Melvin M. Turmin, 386–91. Englewood Cliffs, NJ: Prentice-Hall.

Davis, Kingsley, and Wilbert E. Moore. 1970. "Some Principles of Social Stratification." In *Readings on Social Stratification*, ed.

Melvin M. Turmin, 368–78. Englewood Cliffs, NJ: Prentice-Hall.

Dei, George Sefa. 2012. "Indigenous Anti-Colonial Knowledge as 'Heritage Knowledge' for Promoting Black/African Education in Diasporic Contexts." *Decolonization* 1 (1): 102–19.

Desmond, Adrian, and James Moore. 1991. *Darwin: The Life of a Tormented Evolutionist.* New York: Norton.

DeVault, Marjorie. 1999. *Liberating Method: Feminism and Social Research.* Philadelphia, PA: Temple University Press.

Dickason, Olivia Patricia. 1992. *Canada's First Nations: A History of Founding Peoples from Earliest Times.* Toronto: McClelland & Stewart.

Diski, Jenny. 2008. "Extreme Understanding." *London Review of Books* 30 (7): 11–12.

Doyle, Arthur Conan 1976. *Adventures of Sherlock Holmes.* New York: Schoken.

Duberman, Martin Bauml, Martha Vicinus, and George Chauncey, Jr. 1989. *Hidden from History: Reclaiming the Lesbian and Gay Past.* New York: Penguin.

Durkheim, Émile. 1964. *The Rules of the Sociological Method.* New York: The Free Press.

Durkheim, Émile. 1966. *Suicide.* New York: The Free Press.

Eagleton, Terry. 1990. *The Significance of Theory.* Oxford: Blackwell.

Eagleton, Terry. 1996. *Literary Theory: An Introduction.* 2nd ed. Minneapolis: University of Minnesota Press.

Eagleton, Terry. 2000. *The Idea of Culture.* Oxford: Blackwell.

Edwards, Steve. 2006. *Photography: A Very Short Introduction.* Oxford: Oxford University Press. http://dx.doi.org/10.1093/actrade/9780192801647.001.0001.

Eliot, Nils Lindahl. 2006. *Mediating Nature.* London: Routledge.

Ericson, Richard V., Patricia M. Baranek, and Janet B.L. Chan. 1989. *Negotiating Control: A Study of News Sources.* Toronto: University of Toronto Press.

Fanon, Frantz. 1967. *Black Skin, White Masks.* New York: Weidenfeld.

Fay, Brian. 1975. *Social Theory and Political Practice.* London: George Allen and Unwin.

Firth, Matthew, James Brophy, and Margaret Keith. 1997. *Workplace Roulette: Gambling with Cancer.* Toronto: Between the Lines.

Fraser, Keath. 2002. *The Voice Gallery: Travels with a Glass Throat.* Toronto: Thomas Allen.

Freire, Paulo. 1972. *Pedagogy of the Oppressed*. New York: Herder and Herder.

Frisby, David, and Derek Sayer. 1986. *Society*. London: Tavistock.

Galeano, Eduardo. 2001. *Upside Down: A Primer for the Looking-Glass World*. New York: Picador.

Garfinkel, Harold. 1967. *Studies in Ethnomethodology*. New York: Prentice Hall.

Gillmor, Dan. 2006. *We the Media: Grassroots Journalism, By the People, For the People*. Sebastopol, CA: O'Reilly.

Glass, Julia. 2003. *Three Junes*. New York: Anchor Books.

Gleick, James. 1999. *Faster*. New York: Vintage.

Goffman, Erving. 1961. *Asylums: Essays on the Situation of Mental Patients and Other Inmates*. New York: Doubleday.

Golding, William. 1958. *Lord of the Flies*. London: Faber and Faber.

Gordon, Lewis R. 1995. *Fanon and the Crisis of European Man*. New York: Routledge.

Gordon, Lewis R., and Jane Anna Gordon, eds. 2005. *Not Only the Master's Tools: African American Studies in Theory and Practice*. Boulder, CO: Paradigm Publishers.

Gould, Stephen Jay. 1977. *Ever Since Darwin*. New York: Norton.

Gould, Stephen Jay. 2000. "More Things in Heaven and Earth." In *Alas, Poor Darwin: Arguments Against Evolutionary Psychology*, ed. Hilary Rose and Steven Rose, 101–26. New York: Harmony Books.

Gould, Stephen Jay. 2002. *I Have Landed: The End of a Beginning in Natural History*. New York: Harmony. http://dx.doi.org/10.4159/harvard.9780674063419.

Gramsci, Antonio. 1971. *Selections from the Prison Notebooks*. Ed. Quentin Hoare and Geoffrey Nowell Smith. New York: International Publishers.

Grandin, Temple. 1995. *Thinking in Picture and Other Reports from My Life with Autism*. New York: Doubleday.

Gunter, Barrie. 1997. *Measuring Bias on Television*. Bedfordshire, UK: University of Luton Press.

Hall, Stuart. 1999a. "New Ethnicities." In *Stuart Hall: Critical Dialogues in Cultural Studies*, ed. David Morley and Kuan-Hsing Chen, 441–49. London: Routledge.

Hall, Stuart. 1999b. "The Problem of Ideology: Marxism without Guarantees." In *Stuart Hall: Critical Dialogues in Cultural Studies*, ed. David Morley and Kuan-Hsing Chen, 25–46. London: Routledge.

Harris, Nigel. 1971. *Beliefs in Society: The Problem of Ideology*. London: Pelican.

Hartsock, Nancy. 1998. *The Feminist Standpoint Revisited and Other Essays*. Boulder, CO: Westview Press.

Harvey, David. 1990. *The Condition of Postmodernity: An Enquiry into the Origins of Cultural Change*. Cambridge, MA: Blackwell.

Harvey, David. 2000. *Spaces of Hope*. Berkeley, CA: University of California Press.

Haudenosaunee Confederacy. n.d. "Values." Accessed August 4, 2014. http://www.haudenosauneeconfederacy.com/values.html.

Hobsbawm, Eric. 1983. "Mass Producing Traditions: Europe 1870–1914." In *The Invention of Tradition*, ed. E. Hobsbawm and T. Ranger, 263–307. Cambridge: Cambridge University Press.

Høeg, Peter. 1995. *Borderliners*. Toronto: Seal.

Hyman, Richard. 1975. *Industrial Relations: A Marxist Introduction*. London: Macmillan.

Ionesco, Eugène. 1958. "The Bald Soprano." In *Four Plays*, trans. Donald Merriam Allen, 7–42. New York: Grove Press.

Keat, Russell, and John Urry. 1982. *Social Theory as Science*. 2nd ed. Boston: Routledge & Kegan Paul.

Kelley, Robin D.G. 2002. *Freedom Dreams: The Black Radical Imagination*. Boston: Beacon Press.

Levesque-Lopman, Louise. 1988. *Claiming Reality: Phenomenology and Women's Experience*. Totawa, NJ: Rowman and Littlefield.

Lévi-Strauss, Claude. 1969. *The Raw and the Cooked*. New York: Harper and Row.

Livingstone, David, and Elizabeth Asner. 1996. "Feet in Both Camps: Household Classes, Divisions of Labour, and Group Consciousness." In *Recast Dreams: Class and Gender Consciousness in Steeltown*, ed. David Livingstone and J. Marshall Magna, 72–99. Toronto: Garamond.

Lloyd, David, and Paul Thomas. 1998. *Culture and the State*. London: Routledge.

Lubbe, Hermann. 2009. "The Contraction of the Present." In *High-Speed Society: Social Acceleration, Power, and Modernity*, ed. H. Rosa and W.E. Scheuerman, 159–78. University Park, PA: Pennsylvania State University Press.

Lyotard, Jean-François. 1984. *The Postmodern Condition: A Report on Knowledge*. Trans. G. Bennington and B. Massumi. Manchester: Manchester University Press.

MacKinnon, Mark. 2005. "The War on 'Terrorist.'" *Ryerson Review of Journalism* (Spring): 92.

Marx, Karl. 1969. "Manifesto of the Communist Party." In *Selected Works*, ed. Karl Marx and Friedrich Engels, 98–137. Moscow: Progress Publishers.

Marx, Karl. 1977. *Capital*, vol. 1. New York: Vintage.

Marx, Karl. 1978. "Theses on Feuerbach." In *The German Ideology*, ed. Karl Marx and Friedrich Engels, 121–23. New York: International Publishers.

McNally, David. 2001. *Bodies of Meaning: Studies on Language, Labor, and Liberation*. New York: SUNY Press.

McNally, David. 2006. *Another World Is Possible: Globalization and Anti-Capitalism*. Winnipeg: Arbeiter Ring.

Mehta, Heidi. 2009. "Anti-Racism Glossary." *New Socialist* 65 (1): 8.

Miller, Jody, and Barry Glasner. 2004. "The 'Inside' and the 'Outside': Finding Realities in Interviews." In *Qualitative Research: Theory, Method, and Practice*, 2nd ed., ed. D. Silverman, 125–39. London: Sage.

Mills, C. Wright. 1959. *The Sociological Imagination*. New York: Oxford University Press.

Moran, Dermot. 2000. *Introduction to Phenomenology*. London: Routledge.

Nesbitt-Larking, Paul. 2007. *Politics, Society, and the Media*. 2nd ed. Toronto: University of Toronto Press.

The New Oxford Dictionary of English. 2001. Ed. Judy Pearsall. Oxford: Oxford University Press.

Neuman, Lawrence A. 2000. *Social Research Methods: Qualitative and Quantitative Approaches*. 4th ed. Boston: Allyn and Bacon.

Neuman, Lawrence A. 2009. *Understanding Research*. Boston: Pearson.

Northey, Margot, Lorne Tepperman, and Patrizia Albanese. 2009. *Making Sense: A Student's Guide to Research and Writing*. Don Mills, ON: Oxford University Press.

OED Online. 2009. *Oxford English Dictionary Online*. Oxford: Oxford University Press.

OED Online. 2014. *Oxford English Dictionary Online*. Oxford: Oxford University Press.

Ollman, Bertell. 1993. *Dialectical Investigations*. New York: Routledge, Chapman, and Hall.

Ortner, Sherry. 1974. "Is Female to Nature as Male Is to Culture?" In *Women, Culture and Society*, ed. Michelle Zimbalist Rosaldo and Louise Lamphere, 67–87. Stanford, CA: Stanford University Press.

Orwell, George. 1966. *Homage to Catalonia*. Harmondsworth, UK: Penguin.

Paciocco, David M., and Lee Stuesser. 2008. *The Law of Evidence*. 5th ed. Toronto: Irwin Law.

Palmater, Pam. 2013. "Idle No More: What Do We Want and Where Are We Headed?" *rabble.ca*, January 4. Accessed May 15, 2014. http://rabble.ca/blogs/bloggers/pamela-palmater/2013/01/what-idle-no-more-movement-really.

Parks, Lisa. 2004. "Kinetic Screens: Epistemologies of Movement at the Interface." In *MediaSpace: Place, Scale and Culture in a Media Age*, ed. Nick Couldry and Anna McCarthy, 37–57. London: Routledge.

Parsons, Talcott. 1968. *Sociological Theory and Modern Society*. New York: Free Press.

Pearce, Frank. 2001. *The Radical Durkheim*. 2nd ed. Toronto: Canadian Scholars' Press.

Piercy, Marge. 1979. *Woman on the Edge of Time*. London: Women's Press.

Postman, Neil. 1985. *Amusing Ourselves to Death: Public Discourse in the Age of Show Business*. New York: Penguin.

Proust, Marcel. 1999. *Swann's Way*. Trans. C.K. Scott Moncrieff. New York: Penguin Putnam.

Rankin, Ian. 1999. *Dead Souls*. London: Orion.

Ríos, Alberto. n.d. "Torres-García Map Drawing." *Álberto Alvaro Ríos*. Accessed August 4, 2014. http://www.public.asu.edu/~aarios/resourcebank/maps/page4.html.

Rosa, Hartmut, and William E. Scheuerman. 2009. "Introduction." In *High-Speed Society: Social Acceleration, Power, and Modernity*, ed. H. Rosa and W.E. Scheuerman, 1–29. University Park, PA: Pennsylvania State University Press.

Rowbotham, Sheila. 1973. *Hidden from History: 300 Years of Women's Oppression and the Fight Against It*. London: Pluto.

Sanderson, Douglas. 2013. "Idle. Know More." *Ultra Vires*, February 27. Accessed May 15, 2014. http://ultravires.ca/2013/02/idle-know-more/.

Schutz, Alfred. 1967. *The Phenomenology of the Social World*. Evanston, IL: Northwestern University Press.

Schutz, Alfred. 1978. "Some Structures of the Life-World." In *Phenomenology and Sociology*, ed. T. Luckmann, 257–74. Harmondsworth, UK: Penguin.

Schwandt, Thomas A. 2007. *The Sage Dictionary of Qualitative Inquiry*. 3rd ed. Los Angeles: Sage.

Sears, Alan. 2003. *Retooling the Mind Factory*. Toronto: Garamond.

Sekyi-Otu, Ato. 1996. *Fanon's Dialectic of Experience*. Cambridge, MA: Harvard University Press.

Smith, Dorothy. 1990. "Women's Experience as a Radical Critique of Sociology." In *The Conceptual Practices of Power*, 11–30. Toronto: University of Toronto Press.

Smith, Miriam. 2010. "Social Movements and Media." In *Mediating Canadian Politics*, ed. Shannon Sampert and Linda Trimble, 205–18. Toronto: Pearson.

Sotiron, Minko. 1997. *From Politics to Profit: The Commercialization of Canadian Daily Newspapers, 1890–1920*. Montreal: McGill-Queen's University Press.

Spivak, Gayatri Chakravorty. 1999. *A Critique of Postcolonial Reason: Toward a History of the Vanishing Present*. Cambridge, MA: Harvard University Press.

Steinberg, Dan. 2013. "Notah Begay Calls Redskins Nickname 'Institutionalized Degradation.'" *Washington Post*, February 25. Accessed May 15, 2014. http://www.washingtonpost.com/blogs/dc-sports-bog/wp/2013/02/25/notah-begay-calls-redskins-nickname-institutionalized-degradation/.

Therborn, Goran. 1976. *Science, Class, and Society: On the Formation of Sociology and Historical Materialism*. London: New Left Books.

Thompson, E.P. 1993. "Time, Work-Discipline, and Industrial Capitalism." In *Customs in Common*, 352–403. New York: New Press.

Turner, Bryan S. 2007. "The Constructed Body." In *Handbook of Constructionist Research*, ed. J.A. Holstein and J.F. Gubrium, 493–508. New York: Guilford Press.

Watts, Vanessa. 2013. "Indigenous Place-Thought and Agency among Humans and Non-Humans (First Woman and Sky Woman Go on a European World Tour!)." *Decolonization* 2 (1): 20–34.

Weber, Max. 1958. "Science as a Vocation." In *From Max Weber: Essays in Sociology*, ed. H.H. Gerth and C. Wright Mills, 129–56. New York: Galaxy Books.

Wells, H.G. 1983. *The Time Machine and the War of the Worlds*. New York: Ballantine Books.

Wolf, Eric. 1982. *Europe and the People without History*. Berkeley, CA: University of California Press.

Wolin, Sheldon. 1997. "What Time Is It?" *Theory and Event* 1 (1): 1–10.

Wotherspoon, Terry. 1998. *The Sociology of Education in Canada: Critical Perspectives*. Toronto: Oxford University Press.

Index

corporations, 34, 41–42, 133–34,
165, 174
courtrooms, 58–60, 63, 68, 75, 83
criminality, 144–45
criminal trials. *See* courtrooms
critical social science, 66, 69–70
critical thinking, 9, 14, 50. *See also*
problem solving
cross-examination, 59–60, 75, 83
cultural change, 9
culture, 140–41. *See also* nature/
culture relationship
culture shock, xxii
cycle of inquiry
introduction to, xv
as methodical inquiry, 55
theory in, 3, 9
using, 65–66, 82
See also methodical inquiry

Darwin, Charles, 4–5, 7, 8, 156
Davis, Kingsley, 189–90, 190–91
Dead Souls (Rankin), 120–21
debates, 6–7, 8, 9, 44
decolonization, 20, 199–200
deductive reasoning, 56–57,
65–66, 82
defamiliarization, 15
Dei, George, 18
democracy, 149, 173, 180
denaturalize, 155, 158
Derrida, Jacques, 126, 130
description, 48
Desmond, Adrian, 7
DeVault, Marjorie, 53–54
dichotomization, 155
disadvantaged people
in conflict theory, 30–31, 32,
34, 201
environmental degradation
and, 153
globalization and, 134
as hidden from history, 175
theory for social change and,
191, 192–93

discipline, meanings of, 72–73
disciplined inquiry, 72–73, 74
disciplines. *See* academic disciplines
Diski, Jenny, 53
Disneyland, 132
documentation, 3, 57, 60
"Door of No Return," 12
dreamworlds, 124–25
Durkheim, Émile, 28, 170, 185
*The Rules of Sociological
Method*, 188–89
Suicide, 103–04

Eagleton, Terry, 14, 132, 140–41
ecocentric approaches, 154
ecology. *See* environmental
concerns
economic crisis of 2008–09,
40–44, 137
education. *See* classrooms; learning
Edwards, Steve, 69
Einstein, Albert, 47–48
empirical data, 6, 108
empirical rigour, 47–49
Enlightenment thinking, 35–36
environmental concerns, 151–53,
157–58
Ericson, Richard, 62
eternalization, 149, 150
ethics, 79–81
ethnocentrism, 28–29, 175
ethnomethodology, 117
Eurocentrism, 92
everyday knowledge, 53–54
everyday theorizing, xv–xvi, 3–4,
44–46, 47, 50, 191
evidence, 58–59, 83
evolutionary theories, 4–5, 7–8, 9,
156–57
experts, 63–64, 82
explanations, 25, 26. *See also* theory
extension, 100, 102

facts
in court, 58, 60

consciousness and, 110–11
filtering information with,
108–09, 110, 112–13
See also consciousness;
phenomenology; reality
sexism, 16, 131
sexuality, 140
shopping, xvii–xviii
Silent Spring (Carson), 151
Smith, Dorothy, 93
social change, 9, 30, 190–93
social inequality, 32, 34, 189–191
socialization, 143, 144–45
social order model
on 2008–09 economic crisis,
40–41, 41–42, 42–43
vs. conflict model, xix–xx, *33*
Enlightenment and, 35
functionalism and, 28
globalization and, 30, 133–35
on history, 173
introduction to, 27
on learning, 105–06
in *Lord of the Flies*, 28–29
postmodernist approaches on,
34, 35, 36
premises of, 27, 29, 201
on role of state, 29–30
on social change, 30
on teaching theory, 201–02
theories of knowledge and, 83
social relations, 85–86
social research, 75, 80, 81
social science approaches
core characteristics of, 21
Indigenous knowledge and,
19–20
nature/culture relationship
and, 139
questioning the familiar in,
98–99
sociological imagination
and, 170
social theory
for decolonization, 199–200

empirical rigour in, 48–49
as map for social relations, 85–86
politics of, 187
on reality, 107
social order model and, 29
use of terms in, 5
sociological imagination, 170, 172,
177–78, 180
sociology, 185–86, 188–89
South-Up maps, 97, 98–99
speculation, 48
speed-up. *See under* time
Spivak, Gayatri, 71, 126
standpoint, 15–17
storytelling, 19–20
stratification. *See* social inequality
student debt, 197–98
Stuesser, Lee, 58, 68
Suicide (Durkheim), 103–04
suspension of disbelief, 104
Swann's Way (Proust), 124

Taylor, Frederick, 166
teaching. *See* classrooms; learning
Teena, Brandon, 121
Tepperman, Lorne, 80
theoretical pluralism, 38–39
theoretical thinking
Antonio Gramsci on, 14
approach to, xvi, 3–4
background to book on, xi–xv
introduction to, xv, xxi–xxii
models derived from natural
world, 155–56
practical, 2
purpose of, 2
questioning in, 23–24, 99
research and, xx–xxi, 157
for self-awareness, 144
for understanding concept
frames, 150
use of terms in, 5
as zoom lens, 94–95
theories of knowledge, 64, 72,
83. *See also* critical social